WILLA CATHER *Living*

WILLA CATHER
Living

A PERSONAL RECORD
BY EDITH LEWIS

Foreword by Marilyn Arnold

Ohio University Press
Athens

Library of Congress Cataloging-in-Publication Data

Lewis, Edith.
   Willa Cather living.

   Reprint. Originally published: New York : Knopf, 1953.
      1.   Cather,   Willa,   1873 – 1947 — Biography.   2.   Cather,   Willa,
1873 – 1947 — Friends and associates.   3. Novelists, American — 20th cen-
tury — Biography.   4. Lewis, Edith.
I. Title.
PS3505.A87Z72   1989   813'.52 [B]   88-28901
ISBN 0-8214-0913-1
ISBN 0-8214-0914-X (pbk.)

Contents

Foreword *By Marilyn Arnold*   vii

Preface   xxxiii

Introduction   xxxv

1. Virginia   3
2. Red Cloud   16
3. Lincoln   29
4. Pittsburgh   41
5. McClure's   59
6. Washington Place   74
7. 5 Bank Street   86
8. *My Ántonia*   103
9. *One of Ours*   117
10. *A Lost Lady*   124
11. *The Professor's House*
    and *Death Comes for the Archbishop*   134
12. *Shadows on the Rock*   151
13. *Lucy Gayheart* and *Sapphira and the Slave Girl*   168
14. The Last Years   186

Foreword

IN Jaffrey Center, New Hampshire, in a secluded corner of a church graveyard, are two headstones—one upright and tastefully engraved with a passage from *My Ántonia*, the other modestly flat and plain. The legend on the first indicates that the remains of Willa Cather, 1876– 1947, are buried here. The second indicates that some twenty-five years later the remains of Edith Lewis were squeezed in at the foot of the first grave. That unimposing corner of an old New England graveyard, in the small town where Cather worked a good many summers and autumns, tells a story. Most obviously, it tells what a letter from Cather's sister Elsie to biographer E. K. Brown (25 September [1949]) confirms, that Cather chose burial in New Hampshire rather than Nebraska. Whether she chose to be buried next to Edith Lewis as Sharon O'Brien assumes (356), or whether Lewis made that decision independently, there is something poetically fitting in the fact that the two women, together so long in life, are resting together in death. Still another monument to Cather is the book Lewis wrote, *Willa Cather Living,* reprinted now after thirty-five years.

That New England burial place also makes a statement about the relationship between the two women commemorated there. The size and position of the headstones symbolize not only the relative worldly prominence of the women but also the probable supporting role one played to the other in the daily drama of living. As another of Cather's longtime friends, Elizabeth Sergeant, observes in her more candid memoir, in order to write, "one needed to be alone, . . . or to work in a corner protected by someone who knew what it was all about—like Edith Lewis . . . or Isabelle McClung" (61). Sergeant, a writer herself, describes the relationship between Cather and Lewis as similar to that of captain and first officer (202); and James Woodress, Cather's most distinguished biographer, agrees, pointing out that "Lewis was the one who bought the railroad tickets, made the hotel reservations (usually in her own name to avoid publicity), acted as traveling companion when she could get away from her job, and in general was Cather's 'stand-in'" (200–201). Cather's letters indicate that she pitched in on domestic chores, especially when Lewis was indisposed; but for the most part, Lewis also did the apartment hunting, saw to domestic details, nursed Cather in times of illness, handled routine correspondence when Cather was away, read proofs, mailed manuscripts, ran interference between the world and the writer, and performed countless other services that enabled an artist to do her work.

The erroneous birth date on Cather's headstone, however, reveals the most telling truths about Lewis's nature and the role she played in Cather's life. What the 1876 date hammered in stone, instead of the correct 1873, discloses is Edith Lewis's stubborn loyalty and her determination to serve her friend's memory in the way she believed she was entrusted to do, regardless of truth or convenience. And Lewis knew the truth, at least she knew it by late 1952. In a letter to Sergeant dated 30 November 1952, Lewis admits, "Yes, the 1873 birth date is right. I think there can be no question about it." And in her own memoir, which never announces Cather's birth date, Lewis confesses to it by observing that "in 1883, when Willa Cather was nine years old, her parents decided to leave Virginia" (13). Lewis had twenty-five years to change the birth date on Cather's headstone, but she never did.

Speaking in 1973 at the national seminar honoring the centennial of Cather's birth, Leon Edel rehearsed his delicate negotiations with Lewis on this matter. Selected by the widow of E. K. Brown, the only biographer mandated with Edith Lewis's approval to complete her husband's work, Edel possessed two sensitive pieces of information. He had evidence that Cather was born 7 December 1873, and that her given name was not Willa but "Wilella," after her father's youngest sister who had died of diphtheria as a child. Lewis confessed to both, but would not consent to Edel's revealing the interdictory name. After all, Wilella was abandoned early in the Cather family, in favor of Willie or Willa. Edel agreed not to mention it, provided he could use the correct birth date and footnote the documentary evidence in support of it. In *Willa Cather Living*, however, Lewis chose to perpetuate Cather's invention: "They named her Willa after a son of Mrs. Boak, William Lee Boak, who was killed in the Civil War" (4).

If, as some suppose, Cather took Lewis for granted, Cather's biographers and critics have done her one better. Lewis is mentioned and borrowed from, but only lately has she stirred genuine interest among Cather students and scholars. This quickening of interest makes the reissue of her book a particularly auspicious event. At the time *Willa Cather Living* was first published, in 1953, reviewers mainly observed that this was a simple, personal account of an artist's life written by her dear friend. They were obviously more interested in Cather's achievement than in Lewis's. For the most part, however, the early reviews were favorable, though Maxwell Geismar preferred Brown's work; and Witter Bynner, who knew Cather at *McClure's* and carried his personal grudge against her into his review of Lewis's book, preferred Sergeant's. Geismar calls Edith Lewis "a sort of Alice Toklas to Miss Cather's Stein" (234), while Bynner wonders how Lewis, "who had known [Cather] well," could produce "only this transcript of a life appearing for the most part dogged, dull, artificial" (332). He describes Lewis's memoir as having "the meagre simplicity of a one-fingered melody heard from a determined child" (330). Norman Holmes Pearson, on the other hand, dubs Lewis "the lieutenant and the shield," and insists that "no one else could have set down the life as she knew it" (597).

Noting the unique contribution of *Willa Cather Living*, Caroline Gordon asserts that "present biographers are . . . highly fortunate" to have it (1). Walter Havighurst appreciates it as an "intimate portrait" (49) that contains valuable material absent from Brown's book, and James Southall Wilson is all praise, for both Cather and "her closest friend" (470). The *New Yorker*'s anonymous reviewer perceptively calls the memoir "a pleasant book . . . but—perhaps deliberately—not a very revealing one" (131). Adding his voice to the still rather thin chorus is Alfred A. Knopf, Cather's publisher after 1918. He notes that Cather left "her literary affairs in the devoted hands of her old, old friend Edith Lewis, who was also to receive the royalties from her books. No one could have been more unselfishly devoted to her memory, and every question I had to raise with Miss Lewis in connection with the Cather Estate was answered exactly as Miss Lewis thought her friend would have done had she still been there to speak for herself" (221).

Mildred R. Bennett, whose 1951 book on Cather's Virginia and Nebraska backgrounds broke new ground in Cather studies, knew and published the correct birth date, very likely before Edel had even begun his negotiations with Lewis over the matter. Bennett met with Lewis once, and describes her very much as Edel does—slight of build, intelligent, gracious, and extremely protective of her friend's work and memory. But whereas Edel, who had become the "official" biographer, eventually arrived at friendly relations with Lewis, Bennett never did. Bennett has indicated to me (letter, 3 March 1988) that all went well in this strategic meeting until the conversation turned to Cather. Then, Bennett, says, Lewis became "frantic," twisting a small linen handkerchief "to shreds" and once banging her hand on the table. At one point, she flung out, "Who are you that you think you could write a book on Willa Cather when even I wouldn't?" Of course, then Lewis had not expected to prepare her own memoir, but only to feed notes, memoranda, and selected documents to Brown. From that moment on, Lewis did all in her power to block Bennett's access to Cather family members and others who knew her friend. Nevertheless, Bennett acknowledges that Lewis was "an incomparable help to Cather and she devoted her life to Cather's art." In spite of the fact that she destroyed letters and manuscripts, "she was only trying to carry out what she thought Willa would want her to do. I can't blame her for that loyalty."

It was probably that loyalty, combined with Knopf's encouragement and a fearful distrust of what other biographers might say, that led Edith Lewis to expand the notes she prepared for Brown into a book of her own. In addition, she was disappointed that Brown's widow did not ask her to finish the book to which she had already contributed so much. Certainly, it was not by chance that *Willa Cather Living* came out almost simultaneously with the Brown biography, making Brown's reliance on Lewis apparent in the numerous parallels between the two books. The Sergeant memoir, too, was published in 1953, and the three books were sometimes reviewed together.

Even (or perhaps especially) Elizabeth Sergeant, who knew Lewis personally and had been a guest in the apartment Cather shared with Lewis, experienced frustration in attempting to deal with Edith Lewis. Sergeant's correspondence with Lewis and Brown during the preparation of the Sergeant memoir indicates that she felt obliged to clear most of her manuscript with Lewis before publishing it, and even changed some parts that Lewis found objectionable. Apparently, the biggest bone of contention was over Sergeant's use of her own letters from Cather and the letters of a few others. Writing to Lewis 25 November 1952, Sergeant spends two and a half pages, typed and single-spaced, on the matter. Sergeant points out that "all 'memoirists', as well as biographers, past and present, have checked their memories and extended their horizons through letters. Mr. Brown and I discussed this matter at some length, and its connection with Willa's will. He told me that you had furnished him with a large number of Willa's letters, which he used as background reference, as I have done and paraphrased in places, as I have done."

This same Edith Lewis, who tried to clamp unreasonable strictures on others' use of anything she could construe to be a Cather letter (for example, she vehemently objected to Bennett's publishing some of Cather's childhood writing, claiming it to be epistolary and thus unpublishable under the terms of Cather's will), made free use in her own memoir of the Cather letters at her disposal, notably those to Mrs. A. K. Goudy, whom Cather had known since childhood, and to Ethel Litchfield, a Pittsburgh friend. Moreover, a 2 December 1948 letter to Edith Lewis from one of Cather's nieces, Helen Cather Southwick, indicates that Lewis evidently solicited letters and other papers from family members for Brown to use in his biography; and, no doubt, Lewis found them useful in writing *Willa Cather Living*. It appears, in fact, that she violated the will at least once herself. Lewis reports that Cather's letters from Jaffrey during the fall when she was writing *Lucy Gayheart* were full of pleasure in both the setting and her work. According to Lewis, "When she considered sending the manuscript to New York to be typed, she finally decided not to, because she was 'too afraid of loss in the most registered of mails.' She could never write it again, she declared; the conditions would never again be so good" (174). Surely, Lewis's quotation marks signify not simply paraphrase, but quotation from a letter.

Cather's surviving letters—and there are several hundred, despite her wishes that they be destroyed—offer scant help to the biographer attempting to assess the nature and quality of the relationship between Cather and Lewis. If anything, by the virtual absence of Edith Lewis from most of them, the letters suggest that Lewis played only a peripheral role in Cather's life, or that Cather wanted to create that impression. The former is surely not true; the latter can only be guessed at. Nevertheless, the scores of letters Cather wrote to several close friends over a lifetime, friends such as Elizabeth (Elsie) Sergeant, playwright Zoë Akins, Red Cloud's Carrie Miner Sherwood, and Dorothy Canfield Fisher, frequently allude to

Isabelle McClung but rarely mention Edith Lewis. Furthermore, Cather dedicated some of her work to various family members and friends, but none to Edith Lewis.

When letters to Sergeant, Akins, and Fisher do refer to Lewis, Cather always calls her "Miss Lewis," never "Edith," and she typically says only that Miss Lewis comes or goes, or will come later, or would have forwarded mail. The letters to Sherwood allude to Lewis, and even send occasional greetings from her, but she is never prominent in them. By contrast, in Cather's more reserved letters to friends like Mabel Dodge Luhan and Ferris Greenslet of Houghton Mifflin, she speaks of Edith Lewis as if she were a living, breathing person rather than an appendage or an afterthought. She tells Greenslet, for example, that the already slender Miss Lewis lost several pounds horseback riding and climbing while Cather lost none, that Miss Lewis suffered a relapse in her bout with the flu, and that Miss Lewis prepared at least some of the advertising copy for Cather's books (Knopf thought so, too). Since Lewis traveled to the Southwest with Cather, and even wrote to Luhan on occasion herself, Cather quite naturally speaks freely of Lewis to Mabel Luhan. Curiously, however, even in the Luhan letters, Cather sometimes speaks of "Miss Lewis," though other times she refers to "Edith." This sort of documentary "evidence" (or non-evidence) notwithstanding, surely, the best indication of Cather's regard for Lewis is their long life together, and the genuine affection conveyed in Cather's one surviving letter to Lewis, written from Jaffrey, 5 October 1936. For some reason, this letter escaped Lewis's incinerator. It expresses high-spirited pleasure over the weather and the universe, and it opens and closes with relaxed, habitual tenderness.

Most published views of the Cather-Lewis relationship are, of necessity, based on hearsay, educated guesses, and speculation. In their portrayal of Cather and Lewis in the Northeast, fashioned from recollections and gossip of townspeople, visitors, and neighbors, Marion Marsh Brown and Ruth Crone picture Cather protected and at work while Lewis handled all domestic and secretarial chores. Two recent biographers, Phyllis Robinson and Sharon O'Brien, have ventured to label Cather a lesbian, by their definition a woman whose primary emotional attachments are to other women. They do not unequivocally assume a physical relationship between Cather and Lewis, or indeed, between Cather and anyone else. Nevertheless, for Robinson, Cather's and Lewis's "life together was undoubtedly a marriage in every sense" (208). James Woodress disputes that characterization of the relationship as well as the assumption of lesbianism, and most of Cather's biographers say little about the relationship at all, generally arguing for a stronger, more intense, attachment to Isabelle McClung. They insist that even after McClung's marriage to musician Jan Hambourg, Lewis never replaced Isabelle McClung in Cather's affections. Sharon O'Brien, who accords more importance to the relationship than others have done, regards the bond as "intimate" (354), and believes that although Cather dominated Lewis, the relationship "was not as one-sided as Sergeant describes it" (355). O'Brien suggests, however, that it was not until Cather's death that Lewis dared assert herself. Edel sensed that Lewis had achieved something resembling a "state of curious exaltation" (190) after Cather's death, to be accounted for, according to O'Brien, by Lewis's new sense of "exclusive possession" (356) of her distinguished friend.

Whether they say much about Edith Lewis or not, Cather's biographers are indebted to Lewis, and to *Willa Cather Living,* for substantial amounts of information. The book, if nothing else, is the accomplishment of one who enjoyed inside knowledge. Lewis had undoubtedly heard from Cather's lips the childhood stories that are now part of the Cather folklore, and she learned firsthand the identities of many Cather characters. She also heard Cather assess her own work, and explain its genesis. She knew Cather's tastes in music and books, and her love of humble people and children. She knew, too, of writing begun and not finished, or contemplated and not written. Perhaps even more important, Lewis watched Cather work (or watched over her workplace); listened to her conversation; registered her responses to people, places, events, and circumstances; and nursed her through extremely trying physical ailments and disabilities, including inflamed tendon sheaths on first her right wrist and then her left. Then, too, Lewis accompanied her friend to settings she would use in her fiction, and Lewis describes movingly the writer's response to place. She also observed firsthand Cather's grief over the illnesses and deaths of family members and dear friends, and she knew the toll these agonies exacted from the artist's vital energies and the changes they wrought in her mind.

In view of Lewis's intimate knowledge of Cather, it is surprising that Cather's biographers typically mention Edith Lewis and her memoir merely to document borrowings. Only O'Brien has accorded the book even cursory appraisal, and she concludes that little can be learned about the Cather-Lewis relationship from this "cautious memoir, *Willa Cather Living*. Despite the title," O'Brien complains, "Cather never comes to life—she is Genius observed at a respectful distance. In her zeal to protect her friend's privacy, Lewis gives no sense of the rhythms of their daily life, the reasons for their mutual affection, the domestic and emotional roles each played" (354).

Given the book's legendary biases and its scholarly

deficiencies, it is easy to dismiss both book and writer, to speak instead of Lewis's domination by Cather's personality and art. It is easy to remember my own conversation with Carrie Miner Sherwood twenty years ago in which she said with obvious distaste, "Edith Lewis was nothing but Willie's lackey, just a lackey," and to understand why Sherwood once wrote to E. K. Brown that Lewis "seems to be laboring under some weird obsession." It is easy to point to Lewis's mean-spirited attempts to block Elizabeth Sergeant's and Mildred Bennett's work. It is less easy to judge the quality of a relationship that began in 1903 when the two women met at the home of a mutual friend in Lincoln, Nebraska, a relationship that became so important and comfortable to both that they began sharing living quarters in 1909, and continued to do so until Cather's death in 1947. Obviously, their two careers brought many independent pursuits and frequent separations, often for months at a time. Then, too, Cather's family always had high claim on her affections. Nevertheless, the relationship must have been companionable and satisfying; it appears that neither sought to separate permanently from it. What *Willa Cather Living* reveals is something the most studied caution cannot hide: an unconscious closeness engendered from the customariness of lives lived under the same roof for a great many years.

We acknowledge all of this, but our grudge against Edith Lewis goes deep and is not easily relinquished. We cannot find it in our hearts to forgive her for deliberately, wrongheadedly destroying priceless letters, manuscripts, and other papers. Even so, we would have been yet more impoverished had she not preserved some highly perishable memories in *Willa Cather Living,* and we must acknowledge our debt. There is another debt, too, one that can never be gauged; for who can divine by what fraction Cather's work would have been reduced, in either volume or quality, if Edith Lewis had not created an aura of understanding and a vacuum of protection around her gifted friend?

Although most modern readers wish Edith Lewis had been more honest, or had offered more insights into Cather's books, or had projected a woman instead of an image, *Willa Cather Living* is by all accounts a singularly important book. To the seasoned reader it almost seems a different book now than it did twenty or even fifteen years ago. The recent surge of feminist biography and criticism alluded to earlier has forced a re-examination of Cather's life and work, and of the standard assumptions about them. For the first time, Cather's relationships with some of the women closest to her, notably her mother and a few friends, are under scrutiny; and the possible effects of these relationships on her fiction are being explored. And even though the Lewis-Cather relationship has been largely ignored, the spotlight is slowly, inexorably, turning toward it. As that searching beam draws nearer to Edith Lewis, her book seems uncannily to have erected an anticipatory shield against it, as if she had read the future. Her guarded memoir now appears designed to protect herself as well as Cather. Her gestures of self-effacement—such as the deferential use of "we," the infrequent use of "I," and the calculated use of the full name "Willa Cather" rather than the informal "Willa" or the ultra formal "Miss Cather"—all serve strategically to suggest familiarity at the same time that they preserve distance, from Edith Lewis as well as from Willa Cather.

Granting the importance of other considerations, perhaps the most interesting aspect of *Willa Cather Living* is its subterranean content, what evolved despite all posturing and precautions. This content is the by-product of nearly half a century of inundation in Cather's way of saying things—in conversations, in letters, in drafts of stories read orally, in thousands of pages of proofs, and in repeated readings of the finished works. The narrative voice is ostensibly that of Edith Lewis, for the first time primary author in her own right; but the accents, the rhythms, the tone, and sometimes the words and style, along with the opinions, are unmistakably echoes of Willa Cather, especially the Cather of the letters. Quite frankly, the book is an unconscious symbol of the merging of one mind and life into that of another, the culmination of a process begun fifty years earlier.

This phenomenon, the blurring of authorial identities, adds another level of ambiguity to an already ambiguous book, a book that withholds even as it purports to reveal. Who, after all, is telling the story, Willa Cather in the guise of Edith Lewis or Edith Lewis in the guise of Willa Cather? Or Edith Lewis having come into her literary legacy and now paying homage to the legator? Even when the voices do not combine, a blurring occurs as Lewis sifts reality through the porous image Cather herself helped create. Although Lewis's tabulations of events may be accurate (can we doubt the word of anyone who remembers in 1953 the dress Cather wore on the day of their first meeting fifty years earlier?), her memory was strategically selective, and the figure that emerges from the narrative is still the author's creation. Surely, in some sense that figure is the fictional character Lewis assumed Cather would have created had she written the memoir herself. Then, too, Alfred Knopf's observation that after Cather's death Lewis answered all inquiries in the way that she thought Cather would have responded suggests that Lewis developed a habit of adopting Cather's voice, surely a habit that carried into this book. Lewis's comments on "The Enchanted Bluff," for instance, are distinctly Catherian in flavor and sentiment: "This slight narrative, so unlike anything she had written heretofore, was like an excursion into the future, a tentative foreshadowing of what was to come. It was as if she had here stopped trying to make a story, and had let it make itself, out of instinctive memories, deep-rooted, forgotten things" (70).

Sometimes, the match is much closer, as when in speaking of Cather's Nebraska background, Lewis says, "Perhaps there are certain advantages for an artist in growing up in an empty country; a country where nothing is made, and everything is to be made" (17). Lewis may have intended it, but the echo of Jim Burden's famous first reaction to Nebraska in *My Ántonia* is obvious: "There was nothing but land: not a country at all, but the material out of which countries are made" (8). Later, Lewis appropriates Jim Burden's sentiments about Black Hawk to describe her own reaction to Red Cloud: "It seemed flattened down against the sea of earth as a boat of shipwrecked men is flattened down, almost imperceptible, among the waves. And I felt again that forlornness, that terrible restlessness that comes over young people born in small towns in the middle of the continent; the sense of being cut off from all the great currents of life and thought" (17).

Still later, Lewis compares Cather to "Vicky" (Cather spells it Vickie) in "Old Mrs. Harris" and "Thea Kron-

berg" (Cather spells it Kronborg) in *The Song of the Lark,*
and she does so in language obviously borrowed from the
creator of those characters. As a youngster, she says, Cather
was "pleased with life for the most part, curious and eager
about it, but too intent on her own interests and pursuits
to question it much. But another self had already begun
in her. It was a self that she kept hidden from all but one
or two people. . . ." Describing how, like Thea, Cather
"makes [herself] born," Lewis says,

> She did not even know what she was striving for, what it
> was that had begun to drive and torment her, throwing her
> from one extreme of mood to another, destroying the
> sunny contentment of her childhood. . . . What she was
> chiefly conscious of was a whole continent of ignorance
> surrounding her in every direction, like the flat land itself;
> separating her from everything she admired, everything she
> longed for and wanted to become. (28)

At times the borrowing is simply a phrase or an expression. The reader who recalls Cather's memorable de-
scription of the desert's great echoing cloud mesas in
Death Comes for the Archbishop will recognize the metaphor
when encountering it in *Willa Cather Living.* As Lewis describes her own journey with Cather to Ácoma, passing
the Mesa Encantada on the way, she observes, "A great
cloud-mesa hung over it. It looked lonely and mysterious

and remote, as if it were far distant in time—thousands
of years away" (146).

Granted the correspondences, echoes, and blending of
voices, Lewis's book still offers illuminating truths about
Willa Cather that others might only dimly surmise. For
instance, Lewis can say something like this with personal
authority: "With all her natural ardour and high spirits, I
think that, unperceived by most of the people who knew
her, there was in her also a deep strain of melancholy. It
did not often emerge. Perhaps it even gave intensity to
her delight in things—this sense that human destiny was
ultimately, and necessarily, tragic" (xvii). Further, Lewis
judges that even as a young woman Cather seldom experienced the "lighthearted enjoyment" common in the
young because "she had come to feel life too deeply, and
in too complex a way." Cather was apparently attached
to the past even then: "She never altogether lost the past
in the present—and sometimes the beauty and stimulus
of the new only heightened her nostalgia and regret for
the old. I remember her telling me of her first visit to
Chartres, and of how the wheat-fields of the Beauce filled
her with an almost unbearable homesickness for Nebraska," the same response Cather attributes to Claude
Wheeler in *One of Ours*. Lewis continues, "A letter to
Mrs. Goudy, written from Hyères, has this heartsickness
and longing for old things in every line" (57).

An alert reader can also glean a bit of bonus trivia from *Willa Cather Living*. For example, Lewis indirectly discloses that apparently she and Cather saved their opera "programmes" "from 1905 on" (90), and that Cather kept some sort of a diary. In fact, allowing herself a privilege she would not have allowed another, Lewis quotes from an entry in Cather's "Line-a-day" (184). One other item must be mentioned, too, a tiny gem plucked from Lewis's rather ostentatious parade of celebrities who are said to have befriended Cather during the years when both women worked for *McClure's* magazine. One name, however, she drops for herself instead of for the editorially prominent Cather. Pleading that she has forgotten most of the people who "flowed through the McClure offices," Lewis coyly offers this: "I remember William Dean Howells visiting the place my first year there. He came over to my desk and asked me what I was doing. When I told him, he said in his beautiful voice: 'I was a proofreader too'" (61).

In the end, in spite of all Lewis's efforts at concealing even as she reveals, at distancing both herself and her subject from the reader, we close her memoir with the sense of having experienced a meeting, not only of the two old friends whose lives and affection converge in this book, but also of ourselves with a storyteller. There is an oral quality about *Willa Cather Living*, in the teller who sometimes forgets herself, in the chronology that keeps doubling back to gather in newly remembered events, in the fabrication of a flawless heroine, in the hyperbole of the title. Most of all, there is the teller who, because her tale carries so much convincing truth, would have us believe that it is the whole truth, and that nothing more can be known. But there is also the teller who forgets that graveyards, too, tell tales.

LETTERS CITED

The following letters are in the Beinecke Rare Book and Manuscript Library, Yale University:

Helen Cather Southwick to Edith Lewis, 2 December 1948

Elsie Cather to E. K. Brown, 25 September [1949]

Elizabeth Sergeant to Edith Lewis, 25 November 1952

Edith Lewis to Elizabeth Sergeant, 30 November 1952 (copy)

Carrie Miner Sherwood to E. K. Brown, undated

Letters from Elizabeth Sergeant to E. K. Brown

Letters from Willa Cather to Mabel Dodge Luhan

Letters from Edith Lewis to Mabel Dodge Luhan

Letter from Willa Cather to Edith Lewis, 8 October

1936, Willa Cather Historical Center, Red Cloud, Nebraska

LETTER COLLECTIONS CITED

Letters from Willa Cather to Elizabeth Sergeant, Pierpont-Morgan Library and University of Virginia Library

Letters from Willa Cather to Zoë Akins, Huntington Memorial Library

Letters from Willa Cather to Carrie Miner Sherwood, Willa Cather Historical Center

Letters from Willa Cather to Dorothy Canfield Fisher, Bailey Library, University of Vermont

Letters from Willa Cather to Ferris Greenslet, Houghton Library, Harvard University

WORKS CITED

Bennett, Mildred R. *The World of Willa Cather.* New York: Dodd, Mead & Co., 1951.

Brown, E. K. *Willa Cather: A Critical Biography.* Completed by Leon Edel. New York: Alfred A. Knopf, 1953.

Brown, Marion Marsh, and Crone, Ruth. *Only One Point of the Compass: Willa Cather in the Northeast.* Danbury, Conn.: Archer Editions Press, 1980.

Bynner, Witter. "A Willa Cather Triptych." *New Mexico Quarterly* 23 (Autumn 1953): 330–38.

Edel, Leon. "Homage to Willa Cather." In *The Art of Willa Cather.* Edited by Bernice Slote and Virginia Faulkner. Proceedings of Willa Cather International Seminar. Lincoln: University of Nebraska Press, 1973, pp. 185–204.

Geismar, Maxwell. "The Enchanted Ring." *Nation* 177 (19 September 1953): 234.

Gordon, Caroline. "A Virginian in Prairie Country." *New York Times Book Review,* 8 March, 1953, sec. 7, pp 1, 31.

Havighurst, Walter. "Willa Cather's High Mesa." *Saturday Review* 36 (11 April 1953): 49–50, 64.

Knopf, Alfred A. "Miss Cather." In *The Art of Willa Cather.* Edited by Bernice Slote and Virginia Faulkner. Proceedings of Willa Cather International Seminar. Lincoln: University of Nebraska Press, 1973, pp. 205–24.

Lewis, Edith. *Willa Cather Living: A Personal Record.* New York: Alfred A. Knopf, 1953.

O'Brien, Sharon. *Willa Cather: The Emerging Voice.* New York: Oxford University Press, 1987.

Pearson, Norman Holmes. "Witness Miss Cather." *Yale Review* 42 (June 1953): 595–98.

Review of *Willa Cather Living. New Yorker* 29 (4 April 1953): 130–31.

Robinson, Phyllis C. *Willa: The Life of Willa Cather.* New York: Doubleday & Co., 1983.

Sergeant, Elizabeth Shepley. *Willa Cather: A Memoir.* Lincoln: University of Nebraska Press, 1953. Rpt. Bison Book, 1963.

Wilson, James Southall. "Of Willa Cather." *Virginia Quarterly Review* 89 (Summer 1953): 470–74.

Woodress, James. *Willa Cather: A Literary Life.* Lincoln: University of Nebraska Press, 1987.

Preface

IN 1948, as Willa Cather's literary trustee, I asked Mr. E. K. Brown of Chicago University to write a critical Biography of Miss Cather; and it was to give Professor Brown what material I could for his task that the following narrative was written. I had no thought at the time of ever publishing it. But when Mr. Alfred Knopf, Miss Cather's publisher, saw the notes, he felt that in spite of, or perhaps because of, their personal and informal character, they in a way supplemented Mr. Brown's distinguished work. Because of Mr. Knopf's interest and encouragement, I undertook to add in places to the original draft and prepare it for publication.

I have not tried in these pages to do more than set down the memories and impressions that came to me spontaneously out of my long friendship with Willa Cather; things I learned from Willa Cather herself, and her friends and family, and things taken from my own experience. In doing so, I found how intractable a thing memory is; how it cannot be compelled, but only let alone to follow its own arbitrary path.

The portrait of a great artist, as it finally emerges, must come, I think, from many sources and from many minds. I have written about Willa Cather as I knew her; but with the feeling that it is not in any form of biographical writing, but in art alone, that the deepest truth about human beings is to be found. However that may be, it has been a continuous pleasure to me to renew these recollections; and it is my hope that they may also give pleasure to some of the friends of Willa Cather and her books.

EDITH LEWIS

May, 1952

Introduction

I first met Willa Cather in the summer of 1903. I had come home, having just graduated from an Eastern college, to Lincoln, Nebraska, where I was born and brought up. Willa Cather was spending that summer with her family in Red Cloud. On her way back to her teaching job in Pittsburgh, she stopped off for a few days in Lincoln to visit Sarah Harris, the editor of the Lincoln *Courier,* and it was at Miss Harris' house that I first met her.

Sarah Harris was a very unusual woman for that time and place. Lincoln was probably not more provincial than most college towns of the period: the older women, as I recall it, found innocent recreation in duplicate whist and Browning clubs; the younger ones were lost, mind and soul, in college fraternity activities. In that rather prosaic social atmosphere, where the chief aim in thought was to think correctly, Sarah Harris stood out as a challenging and, to Lincoln people certainly, a most unconventional figure.

She came of one of Lincoln's "best" families. Her brothers, I believe, had high positions in Chicago with the Burlington Railroad, and they may have helped her to finance the Lincoln *Courier*—a weekly— which she not only founded, but of which she was the publisher, editor, business manager, and I think even, when necessity arose, the type-setter.

She was a generous, impulsive, downright, and very emotional person. I remember her bursting into tears once when she was having an argument on politics with my father; it was the first time I had ever seen a grown person cry. She was completely free in her thinking; all her ideas were her own, and she expressed them with an impetuous honesty very refreshing in that rather inhibited society. In the *Courier* she carried on fierce political campaigns, for which she wrote the editorials; she published society items; and she ran a brilliant column of dramatic criticism signed *Willa Cather.*

From the time they first began to appear, I was enthralled by these articles on actors and the stage. I was very much interested in writing; and this writing seemed to have all the qualities I most admired; I felt it to be daring, provocative, original, imaginative; and it gave me a sense of being out in the world, among exciting and momentous things. I used to ask people who Willa Cather was, but never got any very satisfactory answers. In January, 1903, a short story of hers, *A Death in the Desert,* was published in *Scribner's Magazine,* and I read it with fervent admiration. I suppose I must have communicated my enthusiasm to Sarah Harris, for when Willa Cather stopped in Lincoln that summer to visit her, she invited me to come to her house one afternoon and meet her.

How deeply one takes impressions when one is young! In that first meeting I think I felt, without at all formulating it, all that was really essential in what I afterward came to know of Willa Cather.

When the maid showed me into the parlour, Willa Cather and Sarah Harris were having a spirited discussion about something,—I have no idea what—and after I was introduced, they paid no attention to me, but continued their conversation. Willa Cather, a rather slim figure, in a grey and white striped cotton dress, was sitting very upright in a straight-backed chair. She had curling chestnut-brown hair, done high on her head, a fair skin; but the feature one noticed particularly was her eyes. They were dark blue eyes, with dark lashes; and I know no way of describing them, except to say that they were the eyes of genius. I have never met any very gifted person who did not have extraordinary eyes. Many people's eyes, I have noticed, are half opaque; they conceal, as much as they express, their owner's personality, and thought, feeling, struggle through them like light through a clouded sky. But Willa Cather's eyes were like a direct communication of her spirit. The whole of herself was in her look, in that transparently clear, level, unshrinking gaze that seemed to know everything there was to be known about both herself and you.

I had been silent, a fascinated spectator, while Willa Cather and Sarah Harris carried on their duel of words; but when I got up to go, Willa Cather accompanied me to the door, and there she stood and talked with me for fifteen or twenty minutes, giving me her whole attention. She talked to me as if we were fellow-students, both pursuing the same vocation. (Sarah Harris had published one or two of my college themes in the *Courier;* she loved to encourage young people, and besides, she had to fill up her space every week, and had almost no money to pay for contributions; but her Burlington brothers could always get free transportation for her, and she would reward me with passes to Omaha and to Colorado.)

Willa Cather asked me how many hours a day I worked, and what I found the best time of the day for writing; what I liked best to write about. I do not think it was tact, or that she was trying to put me at ease. She had always a warm, eager, spontaneous interest in people. It was impossible for her to make a perfunctory approach to anyone; she wanted at once to get beneath the surface, to find out what they were really like.

I met her once or twice again before she went on to Pittsburgh. She seemed struck by the fact that I was planning to go that Fall to New York to try and get myself a job there—any kind of job. She asked me to stop over in Pittsburgh on my way, and spend a night at the house of Judge McClung, where she was then living.

If I have described this slight encounter at more length than it seems to deserve, it is because it was one of those unimportant incidents that later, when seen from a long perspective, become to one very important. If I had not met Willa Cather at this time, the chances are that I would never have met her, and our long friendship and association, which lasted until her death, would never have happened.

I went to New York that Fall, and rented what was called a "studio" on the south side of Washington Square, and there Willa Cather visited me for a week the following summer. She was working then, when she had any time off from teaching, on the short stories that afterward appeared in her first prose volume, *The Troll Garden*. I had a small job with the Century Publishing Co., and I remember asking her to let me take one of these stories to show an officer of the company whom I knew; but he regretfully though kindly declined it, saying that for the *Century Magazine* they preferred stories "about equally combining humour and pathos."

The following summer (1905) Willa Cather came again to New York, and stayed with me for a longer time. Two of her stories had been published in *McClure's Magazine* in the early months of 1905, and it was probably before her New York visit that S. S. McClure, with his usual enterprise, made a flying trip to Pittsburgh to see her, and arranged to bring out a collection of her stories in book form. It never took Mr. McClure any time at all to make up his mind about people. *The Troll Garden* was published in the Fall of 1905; and in 1906 Willa Cather gave up her teaching job in Pittsburgh, and accepted his offer of a staff position on *McClure's Magazine*.

It was not without some trepidation that she made this change. She was naturally a very fearless person, fearless in matters of thought, of social convention; people never intimidated her; and she was extremely self-possessed in the presence of physical danger. But

ever since her college days, when the crops failed in
Nebraska, and her family were struggling along on
very little money; when in order to complete her
college course she began writing copy at a dollar a
column for the *Nebraska State Journal*—she had known
how hard and humiliating poverty can be. Her first
years in Pittsburgh were years of constant worry about
money; and she was not very confident of ever being
able to make her living successfully. It was dazzling to
think of becoming an editor on *McClure's Magazine* at
a much higher salary than she was then earning; but
how long would it last? Her teaching job was safe and
sure, and she had her summer vacations to write in.

She took a studio for the first few months at 60
South Washington Square, the house in which I was
then living. In 1906, Washington Square was one of
the most charming places in New York. On the north
side the long row of houses of rose-red brick, resi-
dences of aristocratic old New York families, gave it
an aura of gentility and dignity. On the south side,
writers and artists lived. But it was a very sedate
Bohemia; most of the artists were poor and hard-
working. In *Coming, Aphrodite!*, the opening story in
Youth and the Bright Medusa, Willa Cather has recalled
not only the physical aspects of the old studio building at Number 60 and its surrounding neighborhood,

but even more, the youthful, lighthearted, and rather poetic mood of those days before the automobile, the radio, the moving picture—and before two wars. As I look back, it seems to me that young people were younger then—more ingenuous, less initiated. Life seemed more unknown to them—and its possibilities more boundless.

Willa Cather was then about thirty. I think it is her talk that I remember best. It was not that she talked a great deal. She was never a monologist; and one often felt that she enjoyed silence more than conversation. But whatever she said had an evocative quality—a quality of creating much more than her words actually stated, of summoning up images, suggestions, overtones and undertones of feeling that opened long vistas to one's imagination. Her talk was sometimes more brilliant than her writing; for it had the freer quality of improvisation. Thought and language seemed simultaneous with her, as if one did not have to be translated into the other; she rarely had to search or struggle for a word or phrase.

And her voice always took on the colour of what she was saying. It could be harsh, hard, when she felt scornful of something. But when anything moved her deeply, it often had a low, muted, very musical quality. It had many shades and variations. One could usuually tell by the tone of her voice whether she liked, admired the person she was talking to.

I remember her then as brimming over with vitality, with eagerness for life. The city itself, so open to the sea and freedom, the people she met on McClure's, the work she was doing, all stimulated and excited her. She welcomed every new experience with vivid enjoyment. And yet, even then, with all her natural ardour and high spirits, I think that, unperceived by most of the people who knew her, there was in her also a deep strain of melancholy. It did not often emerge. Perhaps it even gave intensity to her delight in things—this sense that human destiny was ultimately, and necessarily, tragic.

Soon after Willa Cather joined the McClure staff, which was then being completely reorganized, owing to the exodus of John Phillips, Miss Tarbell, and their associates, an opening for an editorial proof-reader came about; and Willa Cather urged me to try for it. Will Irwin was then managing editor of McClure's. I applied to him, and was given the job. During the year or more that Willa Cather was working in Boston on the Christian Science articles—her first McClure assignment—I was sent often to Boston to read proofs with her. This was the beginning of our working together. From the time that she wrote *The*

Song of the Lark, we read together the copy and proofs of all her books. It was one of our greatest pleasures.

I stayed on at McClure's until two years after Willa Cather left the magazine, working with Cameron Mackenzie as assistant managing editor: so that in those eight years I came to know well the people and conditions on McClure's, and in what way they affected Willa Cather. About 1909 we took an apartment together on Washington Place, and here she wrote her first novel, *Alexander's Bridge*.

I have tried, in this brief introduction, to trace the outline of how our friendship began. But now I shall go back to the beginning; to the things I have heard from her, and from members of her family, about her Virginia childhood. Some of these things I not only heard, but in some slight degree experienced when, many years later, before she wrote *Sapphira and the Slave Girl*, we made a trip together to Winchester, Virginia, and visited the Back Creek valley country, and the village where Willa Cather was born.

WILLA CATHER *Living*

1 | *Virginia*

WILLA CATHER was born and spent her early childhood on the land her father and her Virginia ancestors for six generations had lived on and farmed.

Her forebears far back, on her father's side, were said to be Welsh; and the name Cather to come from the Gaelic word *cataoir*, meaning *seat*, or *settle by the fire*. There was a legend in the family that during the reign of Charles II two brothers, Bertram and Edmund Cather, as a reward for their loyalty to the Stuart cause were deeded large tracts of land in County Tyrone, Ireland, went to live on these lands, and left descendants; and that one of these descendants came to America and settled in West Virginia. A distant cousin of Willa Cather, Mrs. Annie Cather Darragh, was still living in Donegal County up to the time of Willa Cather's death, and the two often corresponded.

An English ancestor, Captain Jeremiah Smith, also settled in Virginia in the year 1730. In 1762 a large tract of land on Back Creek, Virginia, between Winchester and Romney, was deeded to Captain Smith by Lord Fairfax, who had received from the English crown, when he first came out to the Virginia Colony, a grant of something like five million acres. The Cather family lived on this and neighbouring land down into Willa Cather's life-time. The deed is still among the family papers.

It was Willa Cather's grandfather, William Cather, who bought the farm known as Willowshade, not far from the village of Back Creek, and built there a large three-story brick mansion, with a wing behind, and a white portico with fluted columns, where all Willa Cather's early recollections centered. She was not born in this house, however, but in the house of her mother's mother, Rachel Elizabeth Boak (the original of *Rachel Blake* in *Sapphira and the Slave Girl*). Mrs. Boak was a widow; her husband had been an official in the Department of the Interior, and they had lived in Washington, D. C. after their marriage. But when he died, William Cather bought a house for Mrs. Boak in the village of Back Creek, and Willa Cather's father and mother were living with her at the time their first child was born. They named her Willa after a son of Mrs. Boak, William Lee Boak, who was killed in the Civil War; and it was in memory of this young soldier that Willa Cather wrote the short story and the poem called *The Namesake*.

Willa Cather was probably about three years old when her parents went to live at Willowshade. Her father's older brother George had married a girl from the North, and in 1873 had gone out to Nebraska and taken up land in Webster County. Here the grandfather, William Cather, after a preliminary visit, decided to join him. In 1877 he bought a ranch in Nebraska, not far from that of his son George, and he and his wife Caroline (the grandfather and grandmother in *My Ántonia*) began that new pioneering life in the West which was to become so determining a part of Willa Cather's destiny. He left Willowshade to the care of his younger son Charles.

Charles Fectigue Cather, Willa Cather's father, must have been very attractive as a young man, for he was very attractive as an old man, when I knew him. In person he was tall, fair-haired, and blue-eyed, with extremely gentle, courteous manners. Before his marriage he had read law in a law office in Washington; and because of his kindly and equitable nature, his neighbours in the Back Creek district used often to come to him for help in settling their disputes and advising them in family difficulties. He had a hopeful, friendly disposition; he was perhaps too trustful in his dealings with other men—in her story *Old Mrs. Harris,* which might well have been called *Family Portraits,* Willa Cather has recreated certain aspects of his character, as well as of her mother and herself.

Willa Cather's mother, Mary Virginia Boak, was a handsome, imperious woman, with a strong will and a strong nature. She was always the dominating figure in the family, and her personality made a deep impress, not only on her children, but on her grandchildren as well. In both she seems to have inspired great devotion and great deference—her will was law, to show her disrespect was an unthinkable offense, and her displeasure was more dreaded than any other catastrophe that could happen. She ruled her children with a firm hand—when she punished them, it was no spanking or putting them in a corner; she whipped them with a rawhide whip. None of them ever seem to have borne any grudge for these whippings—always declared they were beneficial. In spite of her occasional severity—even tyranny—she had a most unusual sympathy and understanding of her children's individuality —gave them almost complete freedom, except where the rules of the household were concerned—let them carry out, without interference, all those queer schemes and passionately cherished undertakings that children get into their heads. She had her own absorbing life, and she let her children have theirs. She had a great capacity for caring about things—everything—whether the coffee was hot, whether a neighbour's child was ill, whether it was a good day for the picnic—for caring about living, in fact. Willa Cather always said she was more like her mother than like any other member of the family.

Mrs. Cather had seven children. Roscoe and Douglass, a few years younger than Willa Cather, and a sister, Jessica, were born in Virginia; James, John, and Elsie in Nebraska.

Although some farming was done at Willowshade, the land was poor, and the chief industry on the place was sheep-raising. Willa Cather had a vivid memory of how her father would take her with him, carrying her on his shoulder, when he went to drive the sheep into the fold at evening. Her poem *The Swedish Mother* is a memory of those times. He had a favourite sheep dog, Vic, for whom he made little leather shoes to protect her feet from the sharp rocks; the dog used to come and beg for these shoes. When Mr. and Mrs. Cather decided to move West—when Willowshade was sold, and most of the household furnishings were sold at auction—Vic was left behind, chained up at a neighbour's. But just as the family were taking the train, she came running across the fields, dragging her broken

chain. It was one of Willa Cather's saddest memories
of a time that was all of it tragic for a child of her
nature—loving passionately, as she did, every tree and
rock, every landmark of the countryside, all the familiar
faces, all their "things" at Willowshade, all their ways.

For an active, observant child, very much alive to
everything that went on around her, there were no dull
days at Willowshade. Negroes and poor whites were
employed in the fields and about the house, where
spinning and quilting, butter-making and preserving
and candle-making were carried on by the house-serv-
ants and by old women who came down from Timber
Ridge and North Mountain to help out during busy
seasons. Butchering and curing and sheep-shearing were
done on the place. One of the regular occupations of
the Negro servants, as they sat around the fire on winter evenings, was to cut old materials into narrow
strips, sew them together, and wind them into balls, to
be made into rag carpets by a neighbour woman, a
carpet-maker. The humbler sort of travellers, like the
tin peddler and Uncle Billy Parks, the broom-maker,
were often lodged over night in the wing at the back of
the house. Willa Cather, for whom these casual guests
had an especial attraction, remembered once opening
her tin bank and giving Uncle Billy Parks all the
money in it as a token of her esteem.

A stream of visitors came and went—kinsfolk and friends from Winchester and Washington and the countryside around. The house was often full of guests. Willa Cather's mother was fond of telling one slight episode which indicates, at least, that at a very early age Willa Cather was able to find language to convey her feelings. A little boy cousin named Philip Frederic came with his parents to visit at Willowshade; but it happened at the time that all the spare chambers were full, and there was no place to put Philip Frederic to bed. Willa Cather, although she was then three or four years old, still slept in a cradle; and it was decided that Philip Frederic should have the cradle, and that she should sleep that night in her grandmother's bed. But after the guests left, Willa Cather refused to go back to her cradle. "No, no," she kept repeating mournfully. "My cradle is all Philip Frederic'd up!"

Both Willa Cather's parents were then young and energetic and pleasure-loving. When she was still little more than a baby, they used to ride on horseback to dances, taking her on the saddle with them. Later, when her grandmother Boak came to live at Willowshade, she was left in her care when the parents were away. From the time she was four or five years old, her grandmother Boak used to read aloud to her from the *Bible* and *The Pilgrim's Progress*, and Peter Parley's *Uni-*

versal History. A story from the last seems to have made a curious impression on her. Her parents recalled that she could be kept quiet for long periods by putting one chair upside down on another, and seating her in this imaginary chariot. Here she would sit in complete silence, driving the chariot, while an invisible slave ran beside her, repeating at intervals, *"Cato, thou art but man!"*

One rather alarming incident happened when she was five years old. She was playing by herself in an upstairs room at Willowshade, at some distance from the rest of the household, when a half-witted boy on the place, the son of one of the servants, slipped into the room, showed her an open clasp-knife, and told her he was going to cut off her hand. In recalling it, she said she was very much frightened, but knew instinctively that she must not show she was frightened. She began talking playfully to the lad, and coaxing him to the window, showed him a tall tree that grew outside, its branches almost touching the house. She suggested that it would be very amusing to climb out on one of these branches, and in this way get down to the ground. The stratagem worked, for the boy forgot what he had come to do, and climbed down the tree.

When the old women came from Timber Ridge to make quilts, Willa Cather would creep under the quilting frames and sit there listening to their talk. Mrs.

Anderson, the original of *Mrs. Ringer,* in *Sapphira and the Slave Girl,* was the best of the story-tellers. She knew the family histories of all the countryside, and all the dramatic events that had become legends among the country people. Her talk was full of fire and wit, rich in the native idiom, and many of these stories Willa Cather remembered all her life. Mrs. Anderson had a daughter, Margie, who came to live at Willowshade, partly as a nursemaid, and partly as a houseworker. She was considered "simple" by some of the neighbours; but she had a faithful, loving nature, and a kind of wisdom and discernment about people deeper than practical wisdom. She served the family with perfect self-forgetfulness and devotion. Even as a little child, Willa Cather seems to have understood what it meant to be so utterly humble and defenceless as Margie. She loved Margie with a deep pity and protectiveness, and this feeling never changed. Her most complete portrait of Margie is *Mahailey* in *One of Ours.* But Margie is also *Marty* in her poem *Poor Marty,* and there is something of her in *Mandy* in the story *Old Mrs. Harris,* and in *Sada,* in the chapter *December Night* in *Death Comes for the Archbishop.*

With Margie, Willa Cather used to roam the woods and fields, sometimes going as far as Timber Ridge to visit Margie's mother and listen to her stories. Margie helped her to select calico for the quilts she was set to piece. Willa Cather took great pride in making these quilts. She did the piecing, and the old women quilted them with lamb's-wool from the lambs on the place.

When the family moved West, they took Margie with them, and she lived in their house until her death. Years afterward, in the long, hot Nebraska summers, when Willa Cather went home to Red Cloud for her vacations, she spent a great deal of time working with Margie in the kitchen; making pies and cookies and puddings from old Virginia recipes, and letting Margie "help her." Probably of all the many people of many kinds to whom she gave pleasure in her lifetime, she never gave more absolute happiness to anyone than she did to Margie.

She was a strong, sturdy child, and except for occasional attacks of croup, was rarely ill during those Virginia years. She was not sent to school—her education was her grandmother's reading aloud, and the life and talk that went on around her.

Her Virginia life was one of great richness, tranquil and ordered and serene. With its freedom from all tension and nervous strain, it may have helped to give her that deep store of vitality which underlay her work. When her family sold Willowshade and moved West, she felt the break cruelly. But in later years she believed that for her the move was fortunate. Even as a little girl she felt something smothering in the polite, rigid social conventions of that Southern society—something factitious and unreal. If one fell in with those sentimental attitudes, those euphuisms that went with good manners, one lost all touch with reality, with truth of experience. If one resisted them, one became a social rebel. She told once of an old judge who came to call at Willowshade, and who began stroking her curls and talking to her in the playful platitudes one addressed to little girls—and of how she horrified her mother by breaking out suddenly: "I'se a dang'ous nigger, I is!" It was an attempt to break through the smooth, unreal conventions about little girls—the only way that occurred to her at the moment.

In 1883, when Willa Cather was nine years old, her parents decided to leave Virginia, and join the grandparents, William and Caroline Cather, on their ranch near what is now Catherton, in Webster County, Nebraska, about twenty miles west of Red Cloud. Willa Cather's grandmother Boak went with them, and they all lived together on this ranch for about two years. During much of this period Willa Cather's mother was ill, and the older children were allowed to run about the country much as they pleased. Willa Cather spent a great deal of her time on horseback, riding

about through the thinly-settled countryside, visiting
the Bohemians and Danes and Norwegians who were
their nearest neighbours, tasting the wild plum wine
the old women made, eating watermelons with the
little herd girls, who wore men's hats, and coolly killed
rattlesnakes with clods of earth. Although she did not
go to school, she read many of the English classics
aloud to her two grandmothers in the evenings, and
she learned to read Latin at this time. In a box of
books brought from Virginia she found an old copy
of Ben Jonson's plays, and a set of Shakespeare, and
a Byron. *The Pilgrim's Progress* she read through eight
times one of those winters.

In the first part of *My Ántonia* she has recorded her
own experiences of the land and the people, and there
is a warmth and freshness and triumphant happiness in
that book which springs directly from her own youthful feelings of the time; the joyous awakening to a new
and beautiful country and a thrilling new kind of life.
She gave herself with passion to the country and to the
people, the struggling foreigners who inhabited it; became at heart their champion, made their struggle her
own—their fight to master the soil, to hold the land
in the face of drouths and blizzards, hailstorms and
prairie fires. Many of the friendships she formed in
these years lasted throughout her life.

But it is not in *My Ántonia*, it is in her first novel of the West, *O Pioneers!*, that one hears the first notes of that theme which was to sound again and again, with gathering force, in her later work. She tells how the Swedish girl, *Alexandra*, drove with her brother through the Divide country, the wild land, and felt her new relation to it, a relation that was to become the meaning of her life. "For the first time, perhaps, since that land emerged from geologic ages, a human face was set toward it with love and yearning. . . . Then the great free spirit which breathes across it must have bent lower than it ever bent to a human will before. The history of every country begins in the heart of a man or a woman."

2 | *Red Cloud*

IN some of the trips West that I made with Willa Cather in later years, we would take the Burlington which left Chicago at five in the afternoon, and ride all the next day across Nebraska and Colorado, until in the far distance, toward twilight, faint as clouds upon the horizon, but very different from clouds, more arresting, more assertive, the peaks of the Rockies behind Denver began to emerge, almost like a thought emerging in one's mind.

There were no air-cooling systems then; after leaving Chicago the porter would put a fine screen in one's window, and all night the wind would blow in, full of the scent of sunflowers, of corn fields and ploughed earth. Because of the wire screen, I suppose, the moon would become the center of a great cross of light, hanging above the pastures and fields. The long, swinging motion of the train over the level roadbed gave one the feeling of going West, going home.

On one of those trips West, instead of riding

through to Denver, we changed at Hastings and stopped for a month at Red Cloud.

Perhaps there are certain advantages for an artist in growing up in an empty country; a country where nothing is made, and everything is to be made. Except for some of the people who lived in it, I think no one had ever found Nebraska beautiful until Willa Cather wrote about it. A new convention had to be created for it; a convention that had nothing to do with woods and water-falls, streams and valleys and picturesque architecture. It had not the austerity of the desert nor the majesty of mountains and rivers. There it lay; and it was as new, as unknown to art as it was to the pioneer.

Although I had grown up in Nebraska, I remember how lost in the prairies Red Cloud seemed to me, going back to that country after a number of years; as if the hot wind that so much of the time blew over it went on and left it behind, isolated, forgotten by the rest of the world. It seemed flattened down against the sea of earth as a boat of shipwrecked men is flattened down, almost imperceptible, among the waves. And I felt again that forlornness, that terrible restlessness that comes over young people born in small towns in the middle of the continent; the sense of being cut off from all the great currents of life and thought.

It was this little town, seemingly so insignificant, so commonplace, so meagre in imaginative material, that became for Willa Cather a rich, an almost exhaustless mine of experience. In *My Ántonia, The Song of the Lark, A Lost Lady, One of Ours, Lucy Gayheart* —in many of her short stories, notably *Old Mrs. Harris* —she returns again and again to Red Cloud, just as she herself came back, summer after summer, as long as her parents were alive.

When they left the ranch, the Cather family moved at first into a storey-and-a-half frame house not far from Red Cloud's main street—a house too crowded for that large family of growing children. But it had one feature of enchantment—the attic, a long room with bare rafters, where Willa Cather and her brothers, Douglass and Roscoe, had their three beds, and where in winter snowstorms the snow sifted in through the cracks in the roof and melted on their faces and hair. No one ever disturbed them there, it was their own domain, and it gave them what children need most in the world—the freedom to be alone with their own thoughts and fancies and experiences.

In Red Cloud Willa Cather began for the first time to go to school. She became aware at once that her speech was different from that of the other children, and hastened to get rid of her slight Southern accent.

It was at school, too, that she first adopted the middle name which appears in the early editions of her books. When the other children gave their names at roll call, she hastily improvised for herself the family name of Sibert.

She had the good fortune to come at once under the influence of three very unusual teachers: Mrs. Eva J. Case, a teacher of literature and foreign languages, a woman of winning charm and character—probably the original of *Miss Knightly* in Willa Cather's last story, *The Best Years*; and Mr. and Mrs. A. K. Goudy—Mr. Goudy was principal of the high school when Willa Cather entered it, soon after the family moved to Red Cloud. These three teachers, and Mr. William Ducker, an Englishman of about sixty, a classical scholar who had somehow drifted out to Red Cloud, and with whom she read Latin and Greek, were the people who most influenced her during the years she was going to school and to the Nebraska State University. They were the first persons she had ever known with any intellectual background, any interest in ideas and the culture of the past. She felt that they first taught her to think, first helped her to find her way in the world of imaginative thought, and that she owed to them the early ideals of scholarship and art that gave direction to her own life and work.

Both the Goudys became deeply attached to this new pupil, so unlike the run of Red Cloud boys and girls; with her astonishing familiarity with classical English literature, and her inability to spell correctly; her actual love of Latin, and the great gaps in her knowledge of ordinary things every grade school child knew; above all, with a personality so striking in its originality, daring, vital force, that no one could possibly ignore her; she awakened either strong liking, or hostility and disapproval.

In 1890, when Willa Cather went to Lincoln, to enter the preparatory school of the State University, the Goudys too moved to Lincoln; Mr. Goudy had been elected State Superintendent of Public Instruction, with an office in the Capitol building, and Mrs. Goudy was made Deputy Superintendent. Willa Cather saw them often; and in the summer vacations she wrote to Mrs. Goudy. This correspondence, begun when Willa Cather was fifteen, continued for forty years—until both the Goudys were dead. It was in many ways a remarkable correspondence. Those unguarded early letters, written in a large, immature hand, and filled with the new discoveries she was making about life and people, and about herself—the kind of letters that are only written in the confidence of being infallibly understood—show the crudeness, the extravagance, the occasional bravado of a young, undisciplined talent; and show, too, flashes of rare insight and imagination; a depth of feeling and a capacity for suffering that are found only in exceptional natures.

Equally important to her, but different from her relationship with the Goudys, was that between Willa Cather and Mr. Ducker.

In Red Cloud, Mr. Ducker was familiarly known as Uncle Billy Ducker; but Willa Cather never called him so. Perhaps she felt in this appelation, however affectionately bestowed, something condescending, something that ignored what she considered his superiority over the people who so designated him. For the first time she was becoming conscious of certain very much opposed social values, and for the first time she was definitely taking sides. She never afterward deserted the side on which she then ranged herself.

Mr. Ducker was regarded as a failure, a "dreamer," by the hustling business men of Red Cloud. He made a living for himself and his family by working in a store owned by his brothers; but his real interest was the great Latin and Greek classics, and, curiously enough, scientific experiment. In his house he fitted up a small laboratory, and there Willa Cather used to help him with his experiments. With Mr. Ducker she read Latin and Greek—Virgil, Ovid, the Iliad, some of the odes of Anacreon. And she had long talks with him—about Christianity, about good and evil, about evolution. Mr. Ducker was not a member of any church. He admired Christ, and believed that every man who loved his fellow-men was an incarnation of the Divine. He was not able to believe in personal immortality. In one of their talks he told her about the sacred scarab beetle that was the symbol of power in old Egypt; how it had just as good wings as the eagle, but had burrowed so long in the dirt, its wings had become callous and powerless. "I am content to devote my life to help give the beetle back its wings," he told her.

Willa Cather was perhaps thirteen or fourteen when she first began to read Latin with Mr. Ducker. Her passionate hero-worship of this old scholar was augmented, if anything, after she entered the University of Nebraska, and began to study Latin and Greek under more routine methods. In her summer vacations she continued to read with him. The second summer she noticed that he had begun to fail, and wrote Mrs. Goudy that she was trying to be with him as often as she could. One afternoon she was walking home with him from his store and he said to her, "It is just as though the light were going out, Willie." A few moments after she left him, a child came running after her to call her back. She found Mr. Ducker lying dead on the couch in his living-room, a copy of the Iliad lying open on the floor beside him.

Though study, going to school, seemed to Willa Cather thrilling and important, many other things were important to her too. The country was important. She loved exploring the river country to the south of Red Cloud with her two brothers, Roscoe and Douglass, canoeing with them on the Republican river, which ran between sand bars and sandy banks under low, wooded bluffs; and buggy-riding with them out through the Divide country to visit the old Bohemian and Swedish and German friends they had known on the ranch. Since her father's business was now farm loans and mortgages, farm talk was still a frequent subject of conversation at home. She learned to follow all the changes, the minute details of farming in that country; the plowing, the sowing, the harvesting of each crop, the hazards brought on by weather, the chances, disappointments, triumphs of a farmer's life. She saw the country, not as pure landscape, but filled with a human significance, lightened or darkened by the play of human feeling.

And the people of Red Cloud were important to her. Perhaps the greatest single indication of her artistic gift was her extraordinary sensitiveness to people—

her intense curiosity about them, the depth of her response to them, the way their individuality, their personal traits and behaviour, cut deep into her consciousness, so that years afterward she could summon them
up, not as pale shades, but with all their living colours,
their insistent humanity, to be recreated and given lasting existence through her transforming art. Certainly
the people of Red Cloud were not more interesting
than those of any other small American town. But she
was more interested in them. Perhaps she was more
interested in them even than they were in themselves.
It is they, for the most part, who make up the great
gallery of characters in her books. They and their lives
become the symbols of her own understanding of life,
her loves and scorns, beliefs, appraisals, refusals.

I think she never set out to do a portrait of anyone
as a portrait. Certain people suggested certain situa-
tions, came together in her mind in a composition that
interested her. When it became necessary to change
them in order to carry out her composition, she did so,
much as a modern painter alters, modifies, suppresses
certain features in his subject to suit his conception
and his style.

My Ántonia and *Mrs. Forrester* in *A Lost Lady* are closer,
perhaps, to her remembrance of the actual people than
any other of her characters. *Ántonia*, whose real name

was Annie Sadílek, worked as a "hired girl" for the Miners, a family of Irish Catholic descent, who were the Cathers' nearest neighbours. (The Miner family, and Willa Cather's relationship with them, are pictured in the chapters about the *Harlings* in *My Ántonia;* and the book is dedicated to two of the Miner sisters.) The people of Red Cloud, including the Miner family for whom she worked, never saw anything at all remarkable in Annie Sadílek. She was a good, trustworthy, industrious girl, and people were fond of her; it would never have occurred to them to regard her as a romantic character.

In the same way, it is doubtful if anyone in Red Cloud at that time saw Mrs. Garber, the wife of ex-Governor Garber, in the poetic light of the lost lady of Willa Cather's tale. The hard, biting gossip of a little town drew quite another picture of her. The Garber place, built on a hill across some marshes southeast of Red Cloud, had the prestige the "best place" always has in a small community. Unusual visitors came and went there; it was the target of much comment, some of it admiring, some of it envious and malicious. Willa Cather was one of the children at the picnic described in the opening chapter of *A Lost Lady.* Long afterward she came on an account of Mrs. Garber's death, in a local paper forwarded to New York, and the conception of the novel formed itself instantaneously in her mind.

But perhaps if she had not preserved the same setting and some of the well-known circumstances attaching to Mrs. Garber, few people—so far is the imaginative conception of a character from that of the factual mind—would have recognized that *Mrs. Forrester* and Mrs. Garber were the same.

Of course, in the end it is the imaginative conception which triumphs—which usurps the memory of the other. *Dr. Archie* and *Wunch,* the old music-teacher in *The Song of the Lark,* old *Mrs. Harris* and the *Rosens, Dillon* and *Trueman* in *Two Friends, Ántonia Shimerda* and *Lena Lingard, Mrs. Forrester* and *Captain Forrester* and *Ivy Peters, Claude Wheeler* and his brother *Bayliss, Lucy Gayheart*—these and many others have supplanted, have indeed become their prototypes, even in the memories of those who knew the living figures.

From the time her family first came to live in Red Cloud, legends seem to have gathered about Willa Cather; though it has sometimes occurred to me that these legends are less a reflection of Willa Cather than of the minds of her neighbours and fellow-townsfolk. She was at the age when all young people begin to experiment with life. And perhaps because she was more fearless, less inhibited than the generality of young people, perhaps also because her own family, with a broader tradition than that of many Red Cloud households, looked with tolerance on her proceedings, she did not shrink from—it may be rather enjoyed—challenging public opinion. She wore her hair cut short, in a period when this in itself was the mark of a rebel. She dressed as much as possible like her brothers. She read books like *Anna Karenina* and *Madame Bovary*. She preferred the society of older people, such as the Goudys and the Wieners (a Jewish family of unusual cultivation—the *Rosens* in her story *Old Mrs. Harris*); and especially the society of older men—Mr. Ducker, Shindelmeisser, her German music-teacher, and the two leading doctors of the town, Dr. Damerell and Dr. McKeeby (*Dr. Archie* in *The Song of the Lark*). At one time she was firmly resolved to become a doctor. Her laboratory experiments with Mr. Ducker had turned her mind in this direction—so that when she later went to the University in Lincoln, she wavered between the classical and the scientific course, and finally decided to enter for both, much against the advice of the University authorities. She often accompanied Dr. McKeeby and Dr. Damerell in their long drives about the country to visit their patients; and she learned from them how to administer anaesthetics. I remember the interest with which a famous New York surgeon once listened to her account of how she gave the anaesthetic in the case of a boy whose leg had been badly broken in an accident, and had to be amputated.

Her young childhood had been free, unconscious, almost unclouded. And no doubt her self-portrait as *Vicky* in *Old Mrs. Harris* shows her much as she appeared to her family and neighbours in the early Red Cloud years—good-humoured, confident, self-absorbed—pleased with life for the most part, curious and eager about it, but too intent on her own interests and pursuits to question it much. But another self had already begun in her. It was a self that she kept hidden from all but one or two people like Mrs. Goudy and Mr. Ducker. She has *Harsanyi* say in *The Song of the Lark*— "Every artist makes himself born." For Willa Cather, as for *Thea Kronberg*, it was a slow and painful process. She did not even know what she was striving for, what it was that had begun to drive and torment her, throwing her from one extreme of mood to another, destroying the sunny contentment of her childhood, when, at sixteen, she left home for the first time to enter the preparatory school of the University. What she was chiefly conscious of was a whole continent of ignorance surrounding her in every direction, like the flat land itself; separating her from everything she admired, everything she longed for and wanted to become.

3 *Lincoln*

WHEN Willa Cather entered the University of Nebraska, the institution itself was less than twenty years old. It still had a kind of innocence, if institutions can be said to possess that quality. Boys and girls came there from the farms and small towns, conscious that their parents had made sacrifices to send them, feeling that they must work hard and make haste to learn. The social life among the students was of a very simple, unsophisticated character. If there was something rather bare and bleak about the atmosphere, there was also a great deal of freedom. A student could live, work, think, very much as he pleased, without feeling the pressure to conform to any particular pattern.

I think Willa Cather had no dream or ambition at this time of becoming a writer. She wrote Mrs. Goudy, in the summer of 1890, that she was chiefly interested in astronomy, botany, and chemistry; and though she registered as a classical student, she asked to be allowed to take an examination in chemistry, and passed it so successfully that she was admitted to the Freshman chemistry class. She rented a room in the town and set to work with great seriousness and application, and with great enthusiasm. She had always this power of intense application; one is tempted to wonder, sometimes, where she got it. There was nothing of it in the easygoing, drifting Southern way of her family, who loved to sit about in leisurely conversation, never hurrying to attack the day's business or the day's problems. Viola Roseboro', the head manuscript reader on McClure's, once said that if Willa Cather had been a scrub-woman, she would have scrubbed much harder than other scrub-women. And certainly, in that rather bleak rented room, with the large map of Rome which she bought with her pocket money covering one wall (she describes this room minutely in the Lincoln chapters of *My Ántonia*), she lost, for the first two years at any rate, little time in frivolities. She worked hard at Latin and Greek, standing first in her Latin class of fifty-three students. She got up at five in the morning to study, and worked late into the evenings. She lived very economically. Her room was heated by a small coal-stove, and she carried all the coal for it herself, up two flights of stairs.

It was apparently when she began to write themes for her English classes that the whole direction of her interests took a sharp turn. Her preoccupation with science dropped completely away; and although she went on with her classical studies, the formal methods of teaching Latin and Greek in the classroom, as contrasted with Mr. Ducker's more imaginative teaching, seemed to her lifeless and boring. Even at sixteen, she was not a docile student. The independence with which she undertook to choose, criticize, judge, was later on to bring her into sharp collision—into open warfare, indeed—with one of the chief University authorities.

Her first English teacher at the University was Professor Ebenezer Hunt. Late in the winter of 1890 he assigned his class a study of Carlyle as a subject for their theme work. The theme Willa Cather turned in seemed to him so striking in its eloquence and originality, that without consulting her he arranged for its publication in the *Nebraska State Journal*, where it appeared in the spring of 1891. The editor of the *Journal* wrote an editorial about it; and the talk, the praise, the sudden elevation to fame among her classmates that followed had a marked effect on Willa Cather. S. S. McClure once said: "Never discourage talent. Discouragement hurts talent far more often than it helps." I think the obverse of this was true in Willa Cather's case. It was no doubt injudicious in her professor to rush the immature work of a young student into print. She herself, in later years, was very severe on this sort of proceeding. But perhaps events are sometimes wiser than the minds that try to plan them. From earliest childhood, everything in her life —books, people, places, her own thoughts—had taken the form of imaginative experience. The encouragement and stimulation of this first success seem to have been the spark that released her deepest native impulse into conscious expression.

From then on, most of her energy went into writing. English composition and English literature became her principal studies. In her sophomore year she helped to found and was chief editor of a college paper, the *Hesperian*, to which she contributed editorials, criticism, stories, and plays. It was about this time that she wrote Mrs. Goudy she had decided she could never be a scholar, that she was not meant for that.

These early themes and stories for the *Hesperian* (one or two of which were partly rewritten by her English professor and published, but without her knowledge beforehand, in obscure magazines) had faults which in later years she could be lenient to in others, but found hardest to forgive in herself. They were crude, rhetorical, overwritten, unrestrainedly emotional. They had decided flaws of form, and sometimes of taste. Critics have found in these characteristics merely the first awkward, undisciplined movements of an unusual power and richness of individuality, trying to find its way into expression. But to Willa Cather I think it was always painful to be reminded of these early productions. If they had been allowed to sink back into the obscurity in which she felt they belonged, the fact that she had written a great deal of little value in her school days would not have bothered her. But she bitterly resented, in later life, proposals to collect and publish this student work, which was not protected by copyright—felt that it was merely an attempt to exploit her name for purposes of self-interest. She was sceptical about its having any value for scholarship. In a letter to one professor she used the figure of an apple-grower, who is careful to put only the apples he thinks reasonably sound into his packing-boxes, leaving the defective ones in a heap on the ground. But suppose a neighbour comes along while he is asleep, and puts the worthless apples into the boxes for market? Everyone, she declared, should have the right of supervision over his own work.

In Willa Cather's last two years at the University her mood, and the whole current of her activities, underwent great changes. She was no longer the serious, devoted student, working long hours by lamp-light over her textbooks. She herself said that she did very little studying in these two years, and passed her examinations largely on inspiration. All her forces were concentrated on something different. More and more consciously she was reaching out, not for what her professors proposed to give her, but for what her own instinct told her she needed to have. She read very widely, in both French and English. Her critical faculty perhaps developed more rapidly at this time than her ability in composition. Incidentally, it brought her into what became a dramatic conflict with the head of the English department, Dr. Lucius A. Sherman.

The Sherman method of studying literature was then famous, certainly among the University students and the townspeople of Lincoln, and I think to a certain extent among educators generally. I shall not attempt to describe it, more than to say that it was based on an extremely elaborate analysis of words and phrases, out of which Sherman constructed certain formal laws embracing the whole of literature. I myself, before I went East to college, had the experience of a six months' course in English literature, not under Dr. Sherman, but under one of his assistants, who, I was told, won her doctor's degree by counting the "poetical" words in Shelley. We studied a small textbook of Browning's shorter poems, prepared by Dr. Sherman, with long lists of questions following each poem. Why did Porphyria's lover use her hair to strangle her with? What was the purpose of the last ride together? I do not remember the actual wording, but the questions were of this character.

Whatever the merits of the Sherman system, its faults were those a young, combative, idealistic student would be most intolerant of. The Sherman method, Willa Cather felt, reduced all that was great in literature, the noblest flights of the human spirit, to dry-as-dust, arbitrary formulae. She was not its only foe. Among the club-women and the professorial groups in Lincoln, controversy about it raged. Perhaps one of its greatest benefits was that it made literature, for the time being, as live an issue in the town as politics or social gossip.

Her frequent clashes with Sherman undoubtedly stimulated Willa Cather in forming her own convictions about literary criticism. In 1893 there came an opportunity for her to give these convictions expression in print.

1893 was a very hard year in Nebraska. No one who lived there at the time can ever forget it. For several summers there had been a succession of crop failures throughout the State, and in 1893 a hot wind burnt up the entire corn crop in three days. Banks failed,

Eastern investors drew out all the money they were able to get hold of, farm mortgages were foreclosed. *The Farmers' and Merchants' Bank* in Red Cloud failed, and though Willa Cather's father lost no money in the failure, many men who owed him money did. In addition, Charles Cather was "land poor": he owned a great deal of heavily mortgaged land on which the interest and taxes were mounting up, and nothing was coming in. For a time he was hard put to it to support his family. Willa Cather's two younger brothers began teaching school, in order to help out at home. She herself commenced a course in journalism with Will Owen Jones, the managing editor of the *Nebraska State Journal,* and that Fall began writing literary and dramatic criticism for the *Journal,* at a dollar a column. In the next two years she wrote an extraordinary number of columns.

The theatre had been one of the enchantments of Willa Cather's childhood in Red Cloud. Road companies occasionally stopped there for one-night stands, and Willa Cather and the other children used to read, with thrilling excitement, the billposters announcing them, hang about the railroad station to watch them arrive, and re-live, for weeks afterward, the wonders of *The Count of Monte Cristo* and *East Lynn.* In Lincoln the theatrical standard was high; a great many excellent stock companies came there and gave performances in the old Funk Opera House. Bernhardt in Sardou's *La Sorcière*, Modjeska in *Antony and Cleopatra*, Julia Marlowe in *The Love Chase*, Mary Shaw in *Ghosts*, Richard Mansfield and Mrs. Patrick Campbell, all played in Lincoln in the 1890's. Willa Cather's dramatic column in the *Journal*—full of unexpected and strongly expressed ideas and sentiments, fiery, uncompromising, and above all, intensely personal—soon began to be noticed and talked about among professional theatrical people throughout the West.

Although she greatly enjoyed this work, the high key at which she was living taxed her vitality—inexhaustible as she then felt it to be. After her day at the University she would spend the evening at the theatre, then go over to the *Journal* office and write her review of the play, getting home at one or two o'clock in the morning. Her first meeting with Stephen Crane took place on one of these occasions. He was on his way to the Coast, and dropped into the *Journal* office one night about midnight. He was fascinated by the sight of a young girl—Willa Cather—standing *fast asleep*. He said it was the only time he had ever seen anyone asleep on their feet like that. When she went home after her graduation she wrote Mrs. Goudy that she was dead tired, body and brain.

During her five years at the University she had made the usual enthusiastic student friendships; but her more lasting friendships were, as in Red Cloud, very largely with older people in the town: Mr. and Mrs. Goudy, to whom she used often to go for reassurance and advice; Sarah Harris; the Gere family— Mr. Gere was editor of the *Nebraska State Journal,* and his wife, a woman of great charm and warmth of hospitality, received the young girl like one of her own daughters; the Canfield family; the Westermanns (the *Erlichs* in *One of Ours*). Dr. Tyndale, an uncle of the six Westermann boys, a severe iconoclast, took especial interest in Willa Cather, and in revolutionizing some of her ideas; I believe it was he who at the close of her University career, arranged for her to go to Chicago for a week and hear grand opera for the first time.

Her school friends knew her as uniformly buoyant, self-confident, high-spirited; defiant of conventions (she still wore her hair shingled, at a time when long hair was fashionable, and dressed boyishly); entering with zest into college activities, directing and taking part in college plays, pursuing a great many diverse interests. It was the everyday self one has for the everyday world. But already a part of her had left the college scene and was engaged elsewhere. In *The Song of*

This way of her looks

the Lark there is a passage where she writes of *Thea Kron-berg:* "It was as if she had an appointment to meet the rest of herself sometime, somewhere. It was moving to meet her, and she was moving to meet it."

She had become conscious of life as a struggle, of fierce aspirations, and of the possibility of failure and tragedy, the hardness of human fate. In some of her letters to Mrs. Goudy there is a touching note of self-questioning—touching because of its absolute can-dour; humble, and at the same time fearless. She be-lieved in the power she felt in herself, but she had no soaring illusions about it. She did not know where it would lead, or how far it would take her.

None of the characters in her books is, I think, more purely imaginary than *Thea Kronberg* as a child and young girl. She is not taken from anyone Willa Cather knew. She is drawn partly from surmise as to what Olive Fremstad, the model for the latter part, might have been; partly, perhaps, from a composite of im-pressions about Scandinavians she had known on the ranch. But while the physical personality is entirely different, the person who most resembled the young *Thea Kronberg* in thought, in feeling, in spiritual devel-opment, is Willa Cather herself.

It does violence, I think, to any artistic creation to try to analyse it too closely in terms of personal experience. Whatever its origin, it is new-born; even its author cannot trace how it comes about, by what unconscious process it becomes a living and separate entity. But certainly the essential theme of that novel, the record of how an artist becomes an artist, has its source in Willa Cather's own experiences during these years before she was twenty.

When she went back to Red Cloud after her graduation, she for the first time found herself out of tune with her old surroundings, restless, at a loss, unable to feel her old content in being at home. The financial situation, the obligation to earn some money, weighed heavily on her. She liked nothing that she wrote, and apparently made no attempt to write for publication. She applied for a teaching job at the University, but her application was turned down.

The following year she made a trip back to Lincoln, to visit the Gere family, and while there she met Mr. Axtell, of Axtell, Orr & Co., a Pittsburgh business man. He was planning to bring out a new magazine, to be called *The Home Monthly,* and offered Willa Cather a position as one of its editors. It was the only opportunity in sight, and she accepted it. By the middle of the summer she was living in a room up on the wooded heights of the East End of Pittsburgh, and working assiduously at her new tasks.

4 | Pittsburgh

THE *Home Monthly* was a magazine intended, its announcement said, "for half a million firesides." Its general tone was domestic, didactic, and highly moral. It was a curious place for a young, rebellious mind, impatient of all camouflage, to find itself in. But Willa Cather's first approach to her new work was cheerful and optimistic. The publishers, good business men, though not in any sense literary men, were kind and considerate. They showed great confidence in her—perhaps because of Mr. Gere's impressive account of her abilities. Mr. Axtell went off on a vacation soon after she arrived, leaving her in charge of making up the first two numbers of the magazine. She was elated at being given so much responsibility, and the press of her duties left her little time for introspection. To be earning her living was the most important thing to her just then.

That year, while she was working on the *Home Monthly*, and later, after she joined the staff of the Pittsburgh

Leader, she wrote and published a number of short stories, some of them under her own name, more of them under pseudonyms. They are an indication, I think, of how valueless this sort of writing can be for a truly original writer. They were, to be sure, a kind of practice—but practice in the wrong direction, in doing over and over the kind of thing most destructive to talent. In her college themes she had explored, however crudely and unsuccessfully, her own innate powers and aptitudes; but here she was trying to conform to artificial and mechanical standards which had little relation to her own thinking and feeling. When she afterward gave up journalism for teaching, it might have been thought a retreat from the direction she wished to take. But I think it showed, rather, her knowledge of herself, and her wisdom about the true road for herself as an artist. However much her teaching job drew on her time and strength, it did nothing to compromise her artistic aims. There is a difference in character, almost like a change in personality, between most of the stories she wrote while working for the *Home Monthly* and the *Leader,* and those she wrote after she began to teach— the ones S. S. McClure swooped down on and published in *The Troll Garden.*

At the end of a year, the *Home Monthly* changed hands, and Willa Cather resigned, and joined the staff of a daily newspaper, the Pittsburgh *Leader*. It was probably a better paid job, and certainly a more interesting one. But the three or four years she worked on the *Leader* were, I think, her hardest years. In spite of perpetual homesickness, she would not have wanted to—she could not, in fact—go back to Nebraska. One does not go back. But after the first excitement of being on her own had worn off, she felt herself at a sort of standstill. She was living in cheap boarding-houses, on miserable food, and sending as much money as she could to her family in Red Cloud. She economized on her clothes, and all her personal expenditures. She was temperamentally rather stoical about such things; but the hard grind of newspaper work—her newspaper column often ran to three or four thousand words—left her no energy for anything else. There were times when the sense of the best years of youth going by, and nothing to show for it, no real advance toward the kind of accomplishment she wanted, filled her with discouragement.

George Seibel, in the *Colophon,* has told of the visits she used to make him and his wife at this period—taking a long streetcar ride across Pittsburgh once or twice a week, to read French with him. His wife would put the baby to bed and prepare a little supper; then Seibel and Willa Cather would settle down to the

French classics—Anatole France, Hugo, Gautier, de Musset, Verlaine, Baudelaire, Flaubert. It was one of the few gleams of domesticity in her life just then.

She was writing dramatic criticism for the *Leader,* as she had done for the *Nebraska State Journal,* working later on the telegraph desk. Her weekly article, *The Passing Show,* was also published in the Lincoln *Courier*—where I first saw it. I remember her vivid account of Olga Nethersole, then a young and very gifted actress, as *Carmen.* Describing the love scene with *José,* Willa Cather wrote:

"The celebrated 'Nethersole kiss,' I expected, would be merely a prolonged bit of stage business, rather cheap, perhaps a little vulgar. It was nothing of the sort; it was terrible, if anything; a flash of lightning, an earthquake, anything that terrifies and intoxicates and destroys. Pittsburgh audiences are the coldest you can find anywhere. They do not approve of Miss Nethersole's plays or her realism, but at the end of that act the curtain calls were so many that I lost count of them. ... It is not easy to describe her, this strange English girl, with a physique neither powerful nor imposing, a face by no means beautiful, and a voice that in spite of its emotional range and its hundred unexpected tricks of flexibility, is always just a little harsh. ... She is not pretty, not even good-looking, but she can make you believe anything."

Writing about plays and actors had at least the advantage of taking Willa Cather among people she liked and found interesting. Even the humble and unsuccessful ones lived in a world of artistic standards and endeavour, the world to which she herself naturally belonged. She met with great friendliness among them, a geniality and easy hospitality very grateful to her in the rather bleak life she was then living. She used often to speak of an actress, Lizzie Hudson Collier, who was leading lady in one of the theatrical companies that came to Pittsburgh. This older woman had a warm heart and a generous nature. Willa Cather never forgot her kindness in those days of hardship and struggle, never spoke of it without deep feeling. One incident she told as characteristic of Mrs. Collier. Her company was playing in Pittsburgh, and Mrs. Collier was staying at the Schenley Hotel—then considered very luxurious and splendid. One night Willa Cather dropped in to see her in her dressing-room at the theatre—feverish with a severe bronchial cold, and so hoarse she could scarcely speak. Mrs. Collier insisted on taking her back in her cab to the Schenley, put her to bed in her own room (although she was playing every night, and the cold was in its infectious stage), and nursed her for several days until she was able to be about again.

It is interesting that little trace of her early association with the theatre is to be found in Willa Cather's novels. There is a delightful chapter about a performance of *Camille* in the Lincoln part of *My Ántonia;* a memorable portrait of Modjeska in *My Mortal Enemy*. And at some time during the Pittsburgh period she began a long story, *Fanny,* that had to do with stage folk. But soon after she came to New York she destroyed it. As I remember, it was curiously lacking in her own kind of individuality—as if it had been pushed along by sheer will power, done with the bare surface of her mind.

But another element had come into her life which was to be of deep and lasting influence in her work.

Ethel Litchfield, one of her closest friends in later Pittsburgh years, remembers her often speaking of a newspaper man named Burgoyne, who had the desk next Willa Cather's on the *Leader*. He was musical critic for the *Leader,* and extremely intelligent, not only about music, but about many things. With Burgoyne Willa Cather used to talk a great deal about music.

In that big industrial city where, as she once wrote in her newspaper column, "Wagner is perhaps not so effective as elsewhere, we are all so used to the noise of the iron mills," music was one of the favourite social diversions of the rich. Victor Herbert conducted the symphony orchestra, and brought a great many famous soloists to Pittsburgh. Walter Damrosch came with his company every season, and gave Wagnerian opera for a week. During this week Willa Cather used to attend all the performances, and write about them in her weekly column. She did not attempt to write musical criticism; she knew, and of course knew that she knew, very little about musical composition. She wrote about voices, personalities, dramatic interpretation.

She began to meet a number of musical people, and to make friends among them. Chief of these was Mrs. John Slack, who had a house in Sewickley, Pittsburgh's fashionable suburb, and in this house a large and beautiful music-room, where she often gave musical parties. She was very fond of Willa Cather, and constantly invited her there. Mrs. Slack's next-door neighbours were Ethelbert Nevin, the composer, and his wife, whom Willa Cather met and used to visit. George Seibel tells how she would often bring home one of Nevin's new compositions, and get her landlady, who had a piano, to play it for her.

In a two-part story, published in the *Woman's Home Companion* in 1925, Willa Cather has recalled something of the musical atmosphere she found in Mrs. Slack's house. She called the story *Uncle Valentine*— (*Adagio non troppo*).

Music, for Willa Cather, was hardly at all, I think, an intellectual interest. It was an emotional experience that had a potent influence on her own imaginative processes—quickening the flow of her ideas, suggesting new forms and associations, translating itself into

parallel movements of thought and feeling. I think no
critic has sufficiently emphasized, or possibly recognized, how much musical forms influenced her composition, and how her style, her beauty of cadence and
rhythm, were the result of a sort of transposed musical
feeling, and were arrived at almost unconsciously, instead of being a conscious effort to produce definite
effects with words. All this quite apart from the fact
that music and musicians were so often the chief subject of her books, as in *The Song of the Lark, Lucy Gayheart,*
and *Youth and the Bright Medusa,* and as a minor theme
in *One of Ours* and *My Mortal Enemy.*

She recognized fully her own limitations where
music was concerned—her lack of technical knowledge, which so far as I know, she made no effort to
extend. But she had a very sure intuition of the qualities of music—both its aesthetic and, so to speak, its
moral qualities; its sincerity, or the lack of it, its elevation or vulgarity. She was quickly aware of the
composer's intention, and the character of his style.

In her later years in Pittsburgh, when she was
teaching, Willa Cather never lost this vital association
with music. She was living then with the McClung
family on Murray Hill; and near by, in the same
neighbourhood, were Dr. Lawrence Litchfield and his
wife. Ethel Litchfield had great beauty, and unusual

gifts as a musician. She had gone, at twenty, to Vienna, to study with Leschetizsky, expecting to become a concert pianist. There Dr. Litchfield followed her, and after a whirlwind courtship brought her back a bride. Their house became a center for the visiting musicians who came to the city. They were generously entertained there, and Mrs. Litchfield herself often took the piano part in their chamber music recitals, and played in Pittsburgh concerts. Willa Cather once told her how, before she knew her, she used to stop outside the Litchfield house on her way home from teaching, and stand listening to the music that streamed from it at all hours of the day and night.

In the gay, caressing, tempestuous atmosphere of that house—babies in the nursery, musicians practising furiously in the drawing-room, urgent telephone calls from steel magnates coming in for Dr. Litchfield—he was one of Pittsburgh's most distinguished physicians, and Frick, after he was shot in his office, refused to let any one else attend him— Willa Cather found something intimate, congenial, and extremely enriching. She was often a guest there when some celebrated musician arrived, or when some new composition was to be played. It was one of those close conjunctions with music that she was to make again and again throughout her life.

About 1900 she decided to give up her work on the
Leader, and try for a teaching job. George Seibel speaks
of her at this time as "writing, writing, writing"; but
it was not writing that led anywhere. She knew that,
for her, journalism was a dead end; if she was ever to
develop her particular kind of gift, she would have to
find a certain amount of leisure and solitude. Teaching did not seem to offer a very bright future; but a
teacher at any rate got three months of freedom in the
summer. She went around to different members of the
school board, as applicants had to do, explaining her
qualifications, and was eventually given a position,
first in the Latin department, and later in the English
department of the Central High School.

She must have been a very exceptional teacher of
English. She had, all her life, a great love of children
and young people—from the days in Red Cloud,
when she was the chieftain of her younger brothers
and sisters, leading them into all sorts of adventurous
exploits, to the later years, when she became the companion and friend of her young nieces and her nephew
Charles Cather, and of the young Menuhin children;
bringing to her intercourse with them great imaginative sympathy and tact and wisdom, as well as the wit
and fun and brilliant charm that children love, so that
today there is not one of them who does not speak

of her with profound love and loyalty and regret, as someone incomparable and irreplaceable, who fixed forever certain standards, ideals, values in their own lives.

I remember hearing her give a lecture once to a group of students in the summer school at Breadloaf in Vermont. She walked slowly back and forth in front of the assembly, speaking in a low but perfectly audible voice—she never had any nervousness or self-consciousness in speaking before an audience; while the faces of her listeners had that look of intense absorption one sees at a very exciting play. Her subject, I remember, was Beethoven.

Not long after Willa Cather began teaching, her friend, Mrs. Collier, the actress, came to Pittsburgh in a new play, and she went one night to see her in her dressing-room at the theater. There she was introduced to a tall, handsome girl, Isabelle McClung, who had come behind to congratulate Mrs. Collier on her performance. This chance meeting was to have very important consequences.

Isabelle McClung was the older daughter of Judge Samuel A. McClung, an eminent Pittsburgh jurist, who lived with his wife and children in a large house on Murray Hill. He was a Scotch Presbyterian, a strong and rather formidable character, stern and silent with the members of his family (though he had a certain sardonic humour and perceptiveness), a man of decided intelligence and ability, but with deep and often bitter prejudices. He was very conservative in his tastes, disliking any form of "Bohemianism" or romanticism; hostile toward all radicals. (He was, incidentally, the presiding judge at the trial of Emma Goldman's associate, Alexander Berkman, who tried to assassinate Frick; and gave him the extreme penalty the law allowed.)

His wife was a charming and kindly woman, quite opposed to the Judge in temperament, naturally fond of pleasure and gaiety.

Isabelle McClung had her father's strength of will and character, but as often happens in families, was in violent revolt against his whole tradition, against the whole Scotch Presbyterian attitude toward life. She was very handsome, very much admired in Pittsburgh society; but all her enthusiasms—and they were vehement in the extreme—were directed toward something entirely different from what she met with in her own environment. She admired writers, painters, musicians, actors, foreigners, and the exotic element in life and art. She found Pittsburgh and all her surroundings supremely distasteful and unsatisfying.

Willa Cather, at the time the two met, had already a certain celebrity in Pittsburgh, among people interested in such things, through her dramatic criticism and occasional short stories she had published. From the first Isabelle McClung admired her profoundly:— the warm, frank, radiantly out-going nature that charmed nearly everyone who ever met Willa Cather; her artistic gifts, the sureness and fire of her approach to life and ideas. Here was someone who had the key to everything she herself was seeking. Isabelle McClung, though without artistic talent herself, had a genuine feeling for any sort of artistic accomplishment. Her friendship with Willa Cather gave her life the direction and absorbing interest it had lacked.

She apparently had no difficulty in persuading her father and mother to invite Willa Cather to become a member of the McClung household. Mrs. McClung was naturally kindly and welcoming toward everyone. And even the stern Judge seems to have taken a great liking to Willa Cather from the first, and to have unbent toward her as he did to few people. She found him always a kind and considerate friend.

Living in the McClung house, with its solidity and comfort, its well-trained servants and ordered routine, made a great change in Willa Cather's life. In 1902, through the influence, I believe, of an uncle of Isabelle McClung, she was offered a position in the department of American literature at the Alleghany High

School—a better one than that in the Central High School. Although she still had to get up at six in the morning and take a long, and, in winter, a very cold streetcar ride to and from her work; and although she taught, as she did anything she undertook, with a great expenditure of vital energy, she enjoyed a tranquillity and physical comfort in the McClung house she had probably never before experienced. Isabelle McClung fitted up a sewing-room at the top of the house as a study for her, and she wrote here on week-ends and holidays, and during school vacations; it was here that she wrote most of the short stories that appeared in her first book of prose, *The Troll Garden,* and perhaps a part of *April Twilights,* her volume of verse.

In the early spring of 1902, Willa Cather and Isabelle McClung made their first trip abroad together, travelling first among the little towns along the west coast of England, spending five weeks in London (it was then that she made the famous pilgrimage to A. E. Housman, about which there have been many legends), and after that crossing the Channel and making a short tour through northern France. They stayed five weeks in Paris, boarding with a French family near the Cluny, and from Paris went to Hyères, on the French Riviera, visiting a number of towns in Provence on the way—Nimes, Tarascon, Arles, Avignon. During this trip Willa Cather was writing newspaper articles to help pay her expenses.

This first European journey was, of course, a great imaginative experience. For an artist, who lives intensely in ideas, for whom all the important adventures happen in the mind and spirit, there is nothing quite like that first encounter with European culture on its own soil, in its age-old stronghold—it is a home-coming more deeply moving and transfiguring than any home-coming to friends and family, to physical surroundings, can ever be. And especially so to one born on the far frontiers of the world, where only the faintest trickle comes through of the great traditions, great examples:—a book, *Anna Karenina* perhaps, in paper covers, bought at the corner drugstore; a name, pronounced in a special tone, by some visitor from the outside world; talks with Mr. Ducker in the long summer evenings.

In her last two years at the University of Nebraska, Willa Cather had begun with delight to explore modern French literature. French was then poorly taught at the University; she got little enough from her French classes. But knowing Latin as she did, she found it easy to acquire a fairly fluent reading knowledge of French; and as, one after another, the well-known names became living voices to her, speaking not from the remote past, but with all the fire and immediacy of the modern age, she first began to feel the admiration and love of French art, French form, which has set such an impress on her own work.

On this first trip abroad, it seems to have been the French part of her travels that gave her the greater intellectual stimulus. She had always a strong affection for the English country and the English people. As a people, she admired the English more than any nation, felt a deep blood kinship with them. But I think French culture, coming to it as she did in her most impressionable years, and finding it so new, so challenging and awakening, spoke more directly to her imagination, and more definitely influenced her writing.

Flaubert was her great admiration at this time; and she stopped over in Rouen to see his monument.

In a letter to Mrs. Goudy she speaks of travelling through Alphonse Daudet's country; she found something in the Provençal landscape that deeply stirred her, something that in a hidden way linked itself with the American West. She had read while at school Daudet's *Lettres de mon Moulin,* and had recognized in these sketches a quality and form very sympathetic to her, very suggestive.

On this first visit to Provence one place fascinated her above all others—Avignon. She went back to it many times. It "teased her mind over and over for years," to use Miss Jewett's words. She always wanted to write a story about Avignon; it was the subject of her last, unfinished story.

I think she did not get the lighthearted, unalloyed pleasure from her travels which the sense of holiday and adventure generally gives young people. Light-hearted enjoyment was not often her mood in these years—she had come to feel life too deeply, and in too complex a way. She never altogether lost the past in the present—and sometimes the beauty and stim-ulus of the new only heightened her nostalgia and regret for the old. I remember her telling me of her first visit to Chartres, and of how the wheat-fields of the Beauce filled her with an almost unbearable homesickness for Nebraska; from the train window she saw a little girl riding on a cultivator with her father, and the sight filled her eyes with tears. A letter to Mrs. Goudy, written from Hyères, has this heartsickness and long-ing for old things in every line.

Exaltation, ardour, delight—these she felt often, with an intensity that brought them close to pain. No later experiences ever blurred those first deeply-cut impressions.

In 1903, after her return to America, Richard Badger published her volume of verse, *April Twilights*.

That same year Scribner's published *A Death in the Desert*. In January and May, 1905, *McClure's Magazine* published *A Sculptor's Funeral* and *Paul's Case*. And in the Fall of that year her book *The Troll Garden* was published.

It had been a long apprenticeship. She had known a great many people and a great many kinds of people in her ten Pittsburgh years—actors, musicians, newspaper men, school-teachers, students, society women, a few wandering derelicts, a number of Scotch Presbyterian business men. She had matured greatly in thought and feeling, and in her knowledge of life. But she had arrived only at the threshold of her writing career.

She had at last succeeded in breaking through the conventions, confusions, uncertainties that lie between every artist and his unique vision of reality. In such stories as *Paul's Case, A Wagner Matinée, The Sculptor's Funeral* she had found—not, as the saying is, herself— but that realm of her experience most true, most significant, and most fruitful for her art. After she joined the *McClure* staff, she made various experiments in writing—influenced largely, I think, by the stimulating example of Henry James; he was influencing most young American writers just then. But when she returned to her own undeflected course, it was at a higher level, and with a new freedom, assurance, and power. From *O Pioneers!* on, it took a steadily ascending line.

5 | McClure's

WHEN Willa Cather first arrived at *McClure's*, Miss Tarbell, John Phillips, Ray Stannard Baker, Lincoln Steffens, and several others of the editorial group had already seceded and gone away to found *The American Magazine*. Their exodus had left *McClure's* practically without an editorial staff, and most of the people Willa Cather found there were new. Viola Roseboro', the manuscript reader, had stayed on. Will Irwin, who had done some brilliant journalistic writing—his account of the San Francisco earthquake was much talked about at the time—became the new managing editor. George Kibbe Turner and Burton J. Hendrick joined the magazine as staff writers. Ellery Sedgwick came, but stayed less than a year. Willa Cather was at first associate editor, afterward managing editor. There were a number of experiments with art editors. Howard Pyle held that position briefly—Mr. McClure greatly admired his work; but I think Pyle found the fast and erratic pace of the McClure office too disturbing. T. M.

59

Cleland, elegant and fastidious, for a time put his characteristic imprint on the magazine. Not long after Willa Cather's arrival Mr. McClure gave his son-in-law, Cameron Mackenzie, a position on *McClure's,* so that he could learn the business. When Willa Cather left the magazine, Cameron Mackenzie became managing editor.

Working on *McClure's* was like working in a high wind, sometimes of cyclone magnitude; and of course S. S. McClure was the storm center. In manner he was the gentlest of men. I never saw him lose his temper with anyone, and he was courteous to all alike, from his staff-writers to the office-boys. He could be wonderfully patient with bores, and with dishonest people who were trying to put something over on him. Sometimes, when his patience was unusually tried, he would become a little drier in speech; that was all.

But his electric energy keyed the whole office to a high tension which never relaxed so long as he was in the place; and he seemed to be everywhere at once. Ideas flew from him like showers of sparks. He wanted them all acted on immediately. Some of his ideas were journalistic inspirations, some, of course, were very impracticable; he did not bother to sort them out, he expected his staff to do that. I think they all seemed good to him at the time. He was often criticized, and sometimes ridiculed, by people in the office who could not understand how a man of genius could so outrage their common sense; it gave them a lower opinion of genius. But Mr. McClure had started from nothing at all, and had made a great career, and he had not done it by having inhibitions. He doubtless knew, often enough, that some project he was advocating with great pertinacity could not be carried out; but he liked to play with the idea, to toss it about and catch it again; and seeing how his staff reacted toward it perhaps helped him to make up his mind.

His staff were always "protecting" him; but if this protection was valuable, it was because they had something very valuable to protect. After he lost control of *McClure's*, and was succeeded by a group of hard-headed business men, the magazine never regained its old prestige and success.

A continuous stream of people flowed through the McClure offices; most of them are now forgotten names. I remember William Dean Howells visiting the place my first year there. He came over to my desk and asked me what I was doing. When I told him, he said in his beautiful voice: "I was a proof-reader, too." Ezra Pound stopped in once, on his way, he told me, from Idaho to Italy. He had with him a suitcase full of poems, one or two of which he read aloud to me.

Mr. McClure had a high regard for poetry. He took it seriously, did not use it, like so many magazine editors, to fill up space at the end of a story or article. He published several of the best of Yeats' early poems, and the verse of Kipling, Stevenson, Walter Savage Landor, Henley, Arthur Hugh Clough, and reprints of Walt Whitman and translations of Verlaine frequently appeared in *McClure's*. After Willa Cather came on the magazine, A. E. Housman and Louise Imogen Guiney were added to this list. I recall Mr. McClure saying once that the kind of poetry published by a magazine was an index of its literary quality.

Perceval Gibbon, a young Englishman who wrote a number of brilliant short stories for *McClure's*, often dropped in to see Willa Cather. I remember how she scolded him once for being so supercilious with a poor fellow from out West, who knew a great deal about copper mines, but in trying to write about them encountered almost insurmountable difficulties with the English language. Much of her time was spent in editing just such contributions as his—in taking a mass of turgid, incoherent material and clarifying it, giving it a sequence and a form.

Splendid writing had been one of the glories of the early *McClure's*. Much of Kipling's best work—*Kim* and *Captains Courageous*, and stories from *The Jungle Books*,

The Day's Work, Stalky and Co., Puck of Pook's Hill, and *Rewards and Fairies* were serialized in *McClure's.* Stevenson's *Ebb Tide* was published in the magazine; and Stevenson so far fell under Mr. McClure's spell that he also gave him *David Balfour* to serialize—forgetting that it was already promised to *Scribner's.* (The matter was settled by Mr. McClure taking *St. Ives* instead.) The names of Conrad, Thomas Hardy, Arnold Bennett, Stephen Crane, O. Henry, Jack London, Mark Twain, Conan Doyle, and many others of note appear in these early numbers.

But by 1906, Mr. McClure's enthusiasm had more and more centered on factual material—perhaps because the great story-writers were becoming scarcer. Often some article of unusual journalistic interest would come into the office, but so badly put together, so buried in a jungle of obscuring words, that it took great divination even to recognize that there was anything there. Then Mr. McClure would turn it over to one of his staff writers to disentangle and gather together and erect into some sort of intelligible shape.

At the time of Willa Cather's arrival, excitement about the Christian Science series was at its height. Georgine Milmine had brought Mr. McClure a great mass of highly interesting but badly written and organized material on Mary Baker G. Eddy and the early

history of Christian Science. He was tremendously
stirred up by the possibilities of this material, but saw
at once that it would have to be verified and rewritten. He had different people in the office try their
hand at it, but finally turned the whole thing over to
Willa Cather.

It was a long and difficult assignment. It meant living
in Boston most of that year (1907) and part of the next,
working at intervals with Georgine Milmine, travelling
about New England and interviewing many of Mrs.
Eddy's early associates, looking up records, checking
all facts. Every statement had to be carefully substan-
tiated, for the subject matter was, of course, highly
controversial.

Willa Cather made her headquarters at the old Parker
House—where Charles Dickens had so often stopped
on his American visits. It was then a very pleasant place
to live, with coal fires in the bedrooms, and a large
library, full of beautiful sets of all the classics. Later
she took a small apartment on Chestnut Street, not far
from the studio of that distinguished artist, Miss Laura
Hills, who became one of her dearest and most delightful friends.

She made many congenial friends in Boston. One of
the earliest was Ferris Greenslet, through whose influence Houghton Mifflin became the publishers of her

first four novels. She was often the guest of Mr. Lorin Deland and his wife Margaret Deland, the writer; and it may have been at the Delands that she met Winthrop Ames, then just taking up his career as a theatrical producer, and William Allan Neilson, later president of Smith College, and his beautiful German-born wife.

A friendship she prized deeply was with Louis Brandeis, later Justice Brandeis, and his wife. Through Mrs. Brandeis there came about a meeting that was to have an unexampled influence on her writing career.

In her volume *Not Under Forty* Willa Cather has told how she set out one afternoon from the Parker House to make a call on Mrs. Brandeis; and how Mrs. Brandeis said she wished to take her on farther, to meet "a very charming old lady, the widow of James T. Fields." "Sometimes opening a new door can make a great change in one's life," Willa Cather remarks. This new door was the door of 148 Charles Street. There, in Mrs. Fields' long drawing-room, where so many memorable meetings had taken place, she first encountered Sarah Orne Jewett.

Willa Cather had long known and admired Miss Jewett's work. At that first coming together, there were no preliminaries; they met at once on a level of complete and equal understanding. In addition to the great personal affection that grew between them, they were very sympathetic as artists; they believed in the same things, were in fundamental agreement about good and bad writing. Miss Jewett's health was even then very frail—she died sixteen months later. But during these sixteen months, Willa Cather saw her often, both at 148 Charles Street and at Mrs. Fields' house in Manchester-by-the-Sea, and she visited Miss Jewett and her sister Mary in their house in South Berwick, Maine. They corresponded frequently. Through Miss Jewett's letters there ran a tone of constant solicitude; solicitude for this younger artist whose whole personality had so strongly impressed her, whose true path she felt to be threatened and impeded. Not long before her death she wrote:—

"I cannot help saying what I think about your writing and its being hindered by such incessant, important, responsible work as you have in your hands now. I do think that it is impossible for you to work so hard and yet have your gifts mature as they should—when one's first working power has spent itself, nothing ever brings it back just the same. . . . If you don't keep and guard and mature your force and, above all, have time and quiet to perfect your work, you will be writing things not much better than you did five years ago. . . . Your vivid, exciting companionship in the office must not be your audience, you must find your own quiet centre of life and write from that to the world that holds offices, and all society . . . in short, you must write to the human heart, the great consciousness that all humanity goes to make up. Otherwise what might be strength in a writer is only crudeness, and what might be insight is only observation; sentiment falls to sentimentality—you can write about life, but never life itself. To work in silence and with all one's heart, that is the writer's lot; he is the only artist who must be solitary, and yet needs the widest outlook upon the world."*

I am sure that Willa Cather never forgot this letter. She could not act on it at the time; before she could consider giving up her McClure job, she had to save enough from her salary to live on for a while without distraction. But I think it became a permanent inhabitant of her thoughts.

She put great energy and concentration into her work on the Christian Science articles, and Mr. McClure was delighted with the results. The series was very highly and widely acclaimed—it was a journalistic triumph for the magazine. In 1909 Mr. McClure sent her to England to get material for *McClure's*. There, through William Archer, who became her devoted friend, she

*From *Letters of Sarah Orne Jewett*, edited by Annie Fields, Houghton Mifflin Co., 1911.

met many of the London literary circle—Sydney Colvin, Edmund Gosse, E. V. Lucas, Ford Madox Hueffer, Yeats, Lady Gregory, Wells, and others. She went to plays with Archer, and sat in Yeats' box with Lady Gregory at one of the early performances of the Irish players. There was a gifted young actress in the cast whose beauty and engaging personality vividly impressed her; it was from her that she drew the figure of *Hilda Burgoyne* in her first novel, *Alexander's Bridge*.

She once told a characteristic story of Archer, which she heard from one of his friends. Archer always carried an umbrella with him wherever he went—was never seen without it. One day he and this friend were at the sea-coast after a tremendous storm. The surf was very high, and they, and a crowd of other people, were on the beach watching it. All at once a cry went up that a man was drowning—he had ventured out in the surf and couldn't get back. There was great confusion, people ran to and fro shouting, and Archer and his friend were separated. When the excitement died down, his friend finally found Archer again, fussily hunting for his umbrella; Archer said gloomily that he had put it down for a moment, and now it had disappeared. He seemed much annoyed, and it was with difficulty that he was persuaded to give up the search and start back. On the way his friend suddenly noticed that there was something very strange about Archer's appearance: he was extremely wet—all his clothes were wet!

It was Archer who had gone in after the drowning man and brought him to shore!

The six years that Willa Cather was an editor of *McClure's Magazine* were in many ways very enriching to her. She made more than one trip to London; and at one time Mr. McClure wished to send her to Germany, but she begged off from this. He himself got all his best ideas dashing from place to place, and he enjoyed giving anyone he admired an opportunity to travel.

Mr. McClure's confidence in Willa Cather, and his belief in her talent, her growing success both as a writer and an editor, and the greater freedom and breadth and colour of her life after she left Pittsburgh had, I think, given her a sense of sureness, a happiness of expectation she had not felt before. The disadvantage of her work was, of course, that it was far too stimulating for one of her temperament—and that, as Miss Jewett had warned her, she was using her best years editing a magazine instead of developing as a writer. The McClure office was always a place of conflict, of conflicting personalities. Mr. McClure liked to get very individual people about him, and their individualities did not always harmonize. The atmosphere was gay, exciting, full of mocking humour—and sometimes of a threatening tension. People had always excited Willa Cather; and the continual impact of new personalities, the necessity of talking to and being talked to by so many people, exhausted her nervously. She wrote her old friend Mrs. Goudy that she found the world too big, that one got split up into too many different currents.

She published a number of poems and short stories in *McClure's* in these years; but she herself did not feel that as a rule they reached the level of the best stories in *The Troll Garden*. If so, there was one interesting exception: in 1909 she wrote a brief sketch which she called *The Enchanted Bluff,* and sent it to *Harper's Magazine*. This slight narrative, so unlike anything she had written heretofore, was like an excursion into the future, a tentative foreshadowing of what was to come. It was as if she had here stopped trying to make a story, and had let it make itself, out of instinctive memories, deep-rooted, forgotten things. It was almost like a song without words—so little was it written, so little was set down on the page; just the talk of some young boys around a camp fire at night; yet it was curiously impressive in its suggestion of an intense experience.

To the end of her stay at *McClure's,* Willa Cather's relationship with Mr. McClure was without a cloud. She never flattered him, never compromised her own judgment in order to please him. At the same time she understood and truly admired him; his faults never blinded her to his great qualities. As for him, I think he trusted Willa Cather as he did few people. He had great divination about people; even when he allowed himself to be exploited by them, I think he knew at bottom exactly what they were like. But he enjoyed the adventure of trying new things, enjoyed being free to do rash and foolish things if he chose.

He not only had a great respect for Willa Cather's judgment; he believed absolutely in her integrity, which among the vanities and jealousies and ambitions that so often surrounded him was, I think, a sort of oasis for his restless spirit. And I think also that he found in her something which heightened his pleasure in his magazine—which gave him back his old youthful excitement and pride in being an editor, and made him feel that the game was worth while.

In 1913, after Willa Cather had left the magazine, Mr. McClure asked her to help him write his autobiography. He used to come down to 5 Bank Street, where she was then living, and walk up and down the room, talking it to her. I do not think she made many notes; when he had gone, she would write down what he had said. He never forgot the deep pleasure of this experience—the pleasure of telling the story of his bitter struggles and his splendid triumphs to someone with an ear and an imagination for all it meant to him.

In later years, after the magazine had broken up, and all the staff had gone their separate ways, Mr. McClure would sometimes drop into the office where I was then working, for a half-hour's chat. It was mostly to talk of how much he missed Miss Cather, and how he wished she could help him with the book on government he was writing.

In the winter of 1948-49, after Willa Cather's death, I wished to arrange a meeting between him and Mr. E. K. Brown, Willa Cather's biographer; but I found that Mr. McClure was in a hospital, critically ill, and unable to talk to anyone. He was then almost ninety-two years old.

A month or two later his daughter wrote me that his condition had slightly improved, and she thought it would please him if I were to go and see him. When I visited him in his hospital room, there was very little left of Mr. McClure. But his head on the pillow still had its fine and noble outline, and there was even a slight flush of colour in his skin, which was always fair and delicate. His eyes, instead of being pale and washed-out, as with many old people, were as blue as ever.

It was very difficult for him to bring his consciousness to a focus; it kept drifting off, and I felt that it was only through an effort of pure courtesy that he managed to hold it steady for a few moments. There was great sweetness and patience in the way he would try to speak, try to remember, and then uncomplainingly give up speaking and remembering.

I spoke to him of Willa Cather's book of short stories which had just been published posthumously, and told him it was called "*The Old Beauty and Others.*" All his editorial instinct flashed up. "That's a good title!" he exclaimed, exactly in his old, quick manner. And then he murmured, "She was wonderful—a wonderful girl!"

When I told him we were planning a biography, he said instantly: "I will help you with it!"

A little later an interne came in and asked Mr. McClure how he felt. It took him a moment or two to answer. Then he said: "I think—I am still Mr. McClure."

A week later he died.

6 | *Washington Place*

I believe it was in 1909, after she returned from her first London trip, that Willa Cather and I took a small and not very comfortable apartment together on Washington Place, just off Washington Square. My memories of this time are rather indefinite. I seem to recall it as a period of uncertainty and change, and of somewhat troubled housekeeping. Willa Cather was even then considering whether she ought to leave *McClure's*, and give all her time to writing. We lived very economically. I remember that we discussed once whether it would be worth while to buy a new coffee-pot, since the future seemed so uncertain. Our practice of economy was, however, accompanied by extravagance, and when this is the case, the lack of money does not seem to leave a very deep mark. Even in those days we went often to the opera, sitting high up, in the cheap seats. The Metropolitan, at any rate, was not economizing then. I recall a performance of *Don Giovanni* in 1908, with Eames, Sembrich, Scotti and Chaliapin in the cast, and Gustav Mahler conducting.

It was while we were living on Washington Place that Willa Cather became acquainted with George Arliss and his wife, who had taken an apartment near by. They used often to invite her to after-the-theatre supper parties at their flat—they were very fond of her, very kind and hospitable always, and she loved being with them. She was a warm friend of the Arlisses all her life. Mrs. Arliss used to write to her from England, and in December, 1944, while the war was still on, sent her a cable—"Merry Christmas anyhow!"

Another neighbour was Mrs. Davidge, a daughter of Bishop Potter, a most witty and delightful woman, who had a house near Washington Square. The poet Edwin Arlington Robinson used to come and stay with her for long periods, and Willa Cather often met Robinson there, though she never knew him intimately.

I remember William Archer coming to dine with us one night at Washington Place. After dinner he took Willa Cather to a play, and during the performance *fell fast asleep!*

In those years, as a rule, Willa Cather had buoyant, vivid, sparkling health. But she also occasionally had sudden terrifying illnesses. One winter night, after a particularly enjoyable dinner and evening, she woke up around twelve o'clock with an agonizing earache. The only doctor we knew at this time was the eminent oculist, Dr. Charles H. May, who had formerly practised also as a throat and ear specialist. After she had walked the floor for some time in increasing pain, we decided to go and call on him; I don't think it would have occurred to either of us to ask him to come down. There were, of course, no taxicabs then, and at two o'clock in the morning the streets were dark and deserted around Washington Square. We walked in the wind and bitter cold to a streetcar, and rode uptown to Dr. May's house, where he also had his office; and stood for a long time on his doorstep, ringing his bell and getting no answer. At last lights appeared in an upper window, and Dr. May himself, genial and kind, came to the door. The earache turned out to be mastoiditis, and Willa Cather was in the hospital for several weeks. Before she had fully got back her strength, she went to England again for *McClure's Magazine*.

It was after this second trip to London that Willa Cather began working on a short novel, which was published serially in *McClure's* in early 1912, under the title *Alexander's Masquerade*, and in book form the same year by Houghton Mifflin, and by Heinemann in London, as *Alexander's Bridge*.

In after years, Willa Cather was a very severe critic of this first novel. In a brief article she once wrote for *The Colophon,* she compares it to a "studio picture," and speaks of the impressions she had tried to communicate as "genuine, but very shallow." When Houghton Mifflin, ten years after its publication, asked her for an introduction to a new edition of the book, she wrote:

"Alexander's Bridge was my first novel, and does not deal with the kind of subject matter in which I now feel myself most at home. . . . Everything is new to the young writer, and everything seems equally personal. That which is outside his deepest experience, which he observes and studies, often seems more vital than that which he knows well, because he regards it with all the excitement of discovery. . . .

"When a writer once begins to work with his own material he realizes that, no matter what his literary excursions may have been, he has been working with it from the beginning—by living it. With this material he is another writer. He has less and less power of choice about the moulding of it. It seems to be there of itself, already moulded. If he tries to meddle with its vague outline, to twist it into some kind of categorical shape, above all if he tries to adapt or modify its mood, he destroys its value. In working with this material he finds that he need have little to do with

literary devices; he comes to depend more and more on
something else—the thing by which our feet find the
road home on a dark night, accounting of themselves
for roots and stones which we had never noticed by
day. This guide is not always with him, of course. He
loses it and wanders. But when it is with him it corre-
sponds to what Mr. Bergson calls the wisdom of intuition, as opposed to that of intellect."*

I have quoted this passage at length because it states
what became so rooted a part of Willa Cather's literary faith. For many years I accepted her estimate of
Alexander's Bridge. But in reading it over again, after her
death, I felt that she had never altogether done it
justice. It is true that it is a contrived novel, and one
feels a slightness and an artificiality of structure in the
earlier parts. But when it at last moves into its true
theme, the mortal division in a man's nature, it gathers
an intensity and power which come from some deeper
level of feeling, and which overflood whatever is "shallow" or artificial in the story. It is as if her true voice,
submerged before in conventional speech, had broken
through, and were speaking in irrepressible accents of
passion and authority.

In re-reading *Alexander's Bridge,* I was struck by one

*From *Alexander's Bridge* by Willa Sibert Cather. Houghton Mifflin
Co., 1922.

coincidence: by the way in which, as the story approaches its climax, Willa Cather uses again the symbol of the young boys sitting around a camp fire on the sandbar of a Western river, which had been the theme of *The Enchanted Bluff.* In another form it becomes a chapter of *My Ántonia;* and at last is given its full and magnified expression in *Death Comes for the Archbishop.* And I recalled Vinteuil's "little phrase" in Proust's great work, appearing and reappearing throughout the musician's compositions, until it becomes at last "the masterpiece triumphant and complete."

In the Fall of 1911, after completion of *Alexander's Bridge,* but before its appearance in McClure's, Willa Cather arranged for a several months' leave of absence; and with Isabelle McClung she rented an old house in Cherry Valley, New York—Mrs. McClung's girlhood home, and a place to which Isabelle McClung was deeply attached. Here, during the late autumn and winter she wrote *The Bohemian Girl,* which Cameron Mackenzie, succeeding her as managing editor of McClure's, bought and published in the magazine; and here she also completed a second Nebraska story, begun some time previously, which she called *Alexandra.*

Whether, on her return to New York, she definitely resigned from McClure's, or whether she merely renewed her leave of absence, I do not remember; but

she did not afterward go back to regular work on the
magazine. Early in 1912 she went out to visit her
brother Douglass in Arizona.

Douglass Cather, after doing a great deal of roaming about the Southwest and Mexico, had taken a
position with the Santa Fé railroad, and was stationed
at Winslow, where he lived in a small bungalow with
another railroad man named Tooker. He wrote Willa
Cather urging her to come out and stay with him, and
let him show her something of the country. In the old
summers in Nebraska, he and Roscoe and Willa Cather
had often talked of exploring the Southwest together;
it was one of their favourite projects.

Her first impressions of Winslow, I seem to remember, were not at all romantic. In her letters she wrote of
the piles of tin cans surrounding the town, the flimsy
living arrangements, the general rawness and imperma-
nence of everything. Tooker's talk, his correspondence-
school type of culture, annoyed her—seemed incon-
gruous with his stalwart physique and open Western
countenance. She sometimes took sharp prejudices
against people—and then could suddenly discard them,
wipe them out as if they had never been. In the end she
came to feel that Tooker was one of her truest friends.

With Douglass and Tooker she began to make excursions about the country; and a whole new land-

scape—not only a physical landscape, but a landscape of the mind, peopled with wonderful imaginings, opened out before her. They made one journey to Walnut Canyon, where there were some cliff-dwelling ruins. She had never seen any cliff-dwellings before; but she and her brothers had thought and speculated about them since they were children. The cliff-dwellers were one of the native myths of the American West; children knew about them before they were conscious of knowing about them. How deeply she was stirred by her first actual contact with that age-old but so intensely near and akin civilization, and how the experience of Walnut Canyon took root and grew and flowered in her mind into artistic creation, may be seen in the fourth part of her novel *The Song of the Lark*, which she wrote three years later.

In that book she has also made her amends to Tooker, her brother's railroad friend. As *Ray Kennedy*, he is one of Willa Cather's most sympathetically drawn characters. "He had the chivalry which is perhaps the proudest possession of his race," she writes of him; in that sentence summing up, in a stroke, a judgment that cuts down past all clever comment and satirical observation to the essential quality of the man.

Douglass Cather had travelled enough in Mexico to pick up a fair acquaintance with Spanish, and also to know and like Mexicans. He had Willa Cather's intuitive understanding and sympathy with all kinds of people, and a large tolerance for their differences, their weaknesses and follies. He had many friends among the Mexicans in Winslow,—who were not always kindly regarded by Americans,—among them a very handsome and engaging young Mexican named Julio. Julio took Willa Cather to a number of Mexican dances, and he translated Spanish songs for her, and sang them to the guitar. He is *Spanish Johnny* in *The Song of the Lark;* and the Mexican part of the book is, I think, entirely taken from this time.

Another friend of her brother was the Catholic priest in Winslow. On some of his long drives to distant parishes he would ask Willa Cather to accompany him; and they used to talk about the country and the people, and the old Spanish and Indian legends that still survived. He was the first of many Catholic missionary priests in the Southwest whom she came to know; she often spoke of the tact and good sense so many of them had with their Mexican parishioners, and the cultivation of mind that gave them a long historical perspective on the life in these remote little settlements.

I have spoken of some of the experiences and impressions, on this Arizona trip, which later contributed to Willa Cather's novel, *The Song of the Lark;* but

The Song of the Lark was not in her mind at this time; I think she had no thought at all of it then—it sprang from quite another initial impulse.

She was absorbed, that spring and summer, in two very different ideas.

One of these was the Nebraska story called *Alexandra*, which she had completed during her winter in Cherry Valley. It ran about the same length as *The Bohemian Girl*, but was very unlike *The Bohemian Girl* in theme and treatment. In fact, it was very unlike anything she had done hitherto; she doubted whether anyone but herself would find it interesting. She read it to me before she went West. It began with what is now the first chapter of *O Pioneers!*, and continued, almost unchanged, according to my recollection, through Part I of that story—*The Wild Land*. It ended with a dream the girl Alexandra had—now told at the end of Part III.

She had this story very much at heart; but she was dissatisfied with it. She made no attempt to publish it. I think she felt there was something there which she did not wish to waste by inadequate presentation. If she held it for a while, she might get some new light on it.

She left Winslow late in the spring, and spent June and July with her family in Red Cloud. It was a long time since she had been back in that country with so free a mind. That summer she lived with it as she had done in the days before she became an editor—soaking herself in the scents, the sounds, the colours of Nebraska, the old memories—and a new vision of it all. She began to think about another story, in the same key as *Alexandra,* which she planned to call *The White Mulberry Tree.* Eventually, of course, the two stories came together in her mind and became *O Pioneers!*

O Pioneers! was published by Houghton Mifflin in June, 1913; and Heinemann published it in London. It marked a definite change in her career. The press notices were very favourable. A Philadelphia reviewer wrote: "One seldom finds such perfect restraint, or such a sense of form, in the writing of a woman. We question whether any man, in the whole course of American literature, has produced as good a book as this about the actual soil of our country." The English reviews were especially friendly, and Edward Garnett, who had written introductions for Willa Cather's favourite English edition of Turgenev's novels, declared that it was difficult to praise *O Pioneers!* too highly.

But it was not the acclaim given it by critics, nor the financial rewards—which were very small; for a number of years the sale of her first four novels did not bring in enough to meet her modest living expenses; it was not these, I think, that played much part in forming her decision about the future. It was the feeling that at last she knew the path she wanted to travel. She had found in herself that infallible guide by which, as she wrote later, "our feet find the road home on a dark night."

7 | *5 Bank Street*

DURING Willa Cather's long stay in the West, we had given up our apartment on Washington Place. In the Fall of 1912, while she was still in the West, I started hunting for a new apartment, and was fortunate in finding just the sort of place that suited us at 5 Bank Street.

Five Bank Street was a wide, brick, five-story house which had been built by a rich brewer as a wedding-present to his son, and had later been made, with very few changes, into an apartment house. A wide stair-case ran up through the middle of the house, dividing it into two apartments on each floor. The one we rented was on the second floor above the street. It had seven rather large rooms, with high ceilings, and all the rooms had big windows, facing east, south, and west. The three front rooms we used as one large living-room. It was heated (as was the dining-room) by a coal grate, under a white marble mantel-piece; there was no central heating-system in the house. We bought little copper-lined gas stoves to heat the two bedrooms. The house was lighted by gas, instead of electricity, and in cold weather the gas sometimes froze.

We were delighted with the spaciousness and fine proportions of this apartment, so different from the boxlike place we had on Washington Place. We did not mind certain discomforts, such as having to make our own coal fires and carry coal for them, and having the gas freeze occasionally. The house was very solidly built, with thick walls which shut out the cold in winter and the heat in summer; the man who came to put in our telephone said they were like the walls of a battleship. We got very little noise from our neighbours. Overhead, a German family lived. Their place was thickly carpeted, and the only sound we heard from them was the daughter's practising of the piano in the mornings. She never practised but the one thing—Beethoven's *Appassionata;* but after a while Willa Cather came to like this practising—she said it was like a signal to work, and she associated it with her working hours.

We paid only $42 a month rent when we first moved into this apartment; though afterwards the rent doubled, and then tripled. We lived here from late 1912 until 1927, when the house was torn down, to give place to a more modern apartment building. These were Willa Cather's best working years.

We were also fortunate, not long after we moved into 5 Bank Street, in getting a very unusual French *femme de ménage* to come and work for us. Josephine (her name was Josephine Bourda) was just over from France, and spoke no English. She lived at home, with her father, husband, and one little daughter. They were all rather frightened of America, and suspicious of everything around them. But Josephine came to have confidence in us, and to feel at home with us, and she stayed with us all through the Bank Street years.

Josephine's father had kept a well-known restaurant near Pau, and she herself was a splendid cook, so that at 5 Bank Street we were able to give a great many dinner-parties. She was an important figure in our lives at that time—high-spirited, warm-hearted, impulsive, brimming over with vitality, and intelligent, as the French are; with great humour, very quick perceptions about people, a rather merciless philosophy of life. She would never speak English, and we were forced to speak our very lame French with her. Her personality was so pervasive and uncompromising that she created a sort of French household atmosphere around us; and I think there is no question that this contributed, to a certain extent, to such novels as *Death Comes for the Archbishop* and *Shadows on the Rock*.

We had very little furniture when we moved into 5 Bank Street, but at auction rooms on University Place we bought mahogany chests and a round mahogany dining-room table for a few dollars. Among our possessions were a number of large oriental rugs; and we got some comfortable chairs. An Italian carpenter built us low open book-shelves for our books. Willa Cather found a large etching, by Couture, of George Sand, and had it hung over the fireplace in the living-room—not because she particularly admired George Sand, but because she liked the etching. She had brought back a number of photographs from Italy —copies of Tintorettos, Giorgione, Titians, etc.— and these she now had framed and hung. She also discovered some fine Piranesis at a little print shop which was selling out its wares—she was very much pleased by this find, I remember, and considered them a great treasure.

After we had made the apartment fairly comfortable, we gave no more thought to acquiring new things, or getting better ones than those we had. What money we had we preferred to spend on flowers, music, and entertaining our friends.

We went constantly to the opera at this time. It

was one of the great periods of opera in New York. Nordica and the de Reszkes, Melba and Calvé were still singing during our first years in New York. From 1905 on our old programmes continually list such names as Sembrich, Farrar, Chaliapin, Plançon, Destinn, Renaud, Mary Garden, Caruso, Amato, Homer, and Tetrazzini. Toscanini, not then half so famous, but at the height of his powers, was conducting two or three times a week at the Metropolitan. But the most thrilling, to us, of all the new stars that came up over the horizon was Olive Fremstad. We heard her nearly every time she sang.

It was not only as a great singer and actress that one admired Fremstad: she was above all a great artist, a great visionary in art. One felt always that her vision was greater than any human power could encompass or satisfy. I think it was her unresting, unappeasable aspiration that gave Fremstad's genius its unique quality, and its power over her audiences. Her voice, though very individual, was not a great voice in the sense that Caruso's was. Many critics said she had injured her voice and shortened her singing career, by making it from a contralto into a soprano. She herself said it was always a mezzo-soprano.

In 1913 Cameron Mackenzie asked Willa Cather to do an article on the opera for *McClure's,* and she wrote

one called *Three American Singers,* which was published
in December, 1913. The three singers were Homer, Farrar, and Olive Fremstad, and she interviewed each of
them. Her first meeting with Fremstad was a curious
one. It took place in this way:—

Fremstad had given her a late afternoon appointment at her apartment near Riverside Drive. Willa
Cather was to interview her there, pick up a hasty
supper somewhere, and join Isabelle McClung (who
was visiting us) and me at the Metropolitan Opera
House, for we had tickets for *Tales of Hoffmann* that
evening. But when she arrived, just before the curtain
went up, she told us, to our great disappointment,
that the interview had not come off.

She had gone to Fremstad's apartment—waited—
Fremstad was away on a motor ride, and there was
some delay about getting back. Finally she came in,
very tired, and began at once to apologize; but she
could scarcely speak—her voice was just a husky whis-
per. She was pale, drawn— "Why, she looked forty
years old!" Willa Cather told us. She begged Fremstad
not to try to talk—said she would come back for the
interview another time, and left.

This was all she had time to tell us before the
opera began.

The second act of *Tales of Hoffmann* is of course the

Venetian scene. The intermission seemed very long, and the audience got very restless. Finally the manager came out before the curtain. The soprano, he announced, had been taken ill, and would be unable to appear; but Mme. Olive Fremstad had kindly consented to sing in her place. Then the curtain went up —and there, before our astonished eyes, was Fremstad—whom Willa Cather had left only an hour before—now a vision of dazzling youth and beauty. She sang that night in a voice so opulent, so effortless, that it seemed as if she were dreaming the music, not singing it.

"But it's impossible," Willa Cather kept saying. "It's impossible."

She saw Mme. Fremstad frequently after that. Fremstad came to Bank Street a number of times for dinner, and Willa Cather often had tea with her at her apartment. In June, 1914, she visited Fremstad for a few days at her summer place near Bridgeport, Maine. It was her intense preoccupation with opera at that time, and her great admiration for Mme. Fremstad, and interest in her complex personality, that gave the core of its inspiration to *The Song of the Lark*. I have noted elsewhere in this narrative that *Thea* is not a portrait of Fremstad—that many other elements enter into the character, especially much of Willa Cather's own childhood and youth; but *Thea* as a singer, and particularly in the latter part of the book, was directly suggested by Fremstad. She herself recognized herself in *Thea* when she read the story, and at their next meeting flung her arms about Willa Cather, exclaiming that she could not tell where *Thea* left off and she began.

The *Song of the Lark* was published in 1915. Although Willa Cather was inclined to be critical of it in later years, it was a book that she took great pleasure in writing. She was working under happier conditions than ever before—her life and her work were perhaps for the first time in harmony. She felt settled and secure at 5 Bank Street—liked her surroundings, and found it a good place to write. Her time was all her own, and she had got over her first nervousness at not earning a salary. And all the outside elements of life, particularly the atmosphere of music in which she was living then, and her two journeys West (she made a second trip in 1914) were intensely stimulating to her imagination.

Perhaps the faults she found in this book came in part from working too directly from immediate emotions and impressions. I think no other of her novels was written in this way.

In the summer of 1915 we made our first trip together to the Southwest. We took the Burlington

from Chicago, and rode all one day across Nebraska
and the Colorado desert to Denver. I remember how,
from the train windows, we followed the Republican
River—the river of Willa Cather's Red Cloud childhood—to its source, as it wound like a snake back
and forth from one side of the tracks to the other;
and how the orange milkweed was in bloom all along
the way. Willa Cather had long wished to visit the
Mesa Verde, in the southwestern corner of Colorado;
so from Denver we travelled by the wonderful nar-
row-gauge road of the Denver and Rio Grande, up
through La Veta pass and over the Continental Divide to Durango, and from Durango to Mancos—
sitting much of the way on the open back platform
of the little wooden train, where we could see the
engine puffing ahead around the curves.

Mancos is about twenty miles from the Mesa Verde. I do not remember seeing any automobiles in
that country then—but in any case, there was no road
up the Mesa Verde that an automobile could travel,
and we engaged a team and driver to take us there.
Willa Cather had heard that one of the Wetherill
family, a brother of the Dick Wetherill who first
"discovered" the Mesa Verde, was still living in
Mancos, and on the evening before we started for
the Mesa she went to call on him; and from him she

heard the whole story of how Dick Wetherill swam
the Mancos river on his horse and rode into the Mesa
after lost cattle, and how he came upon the cliff
dwellings that had been hidden there for centuries.

We spent a week on the Mesa Verde. Very few
people visited the place then—we were, I think, the
only guests for the greater part of that week—and
the forest ranger and guide, a young man named Jeep,
who ran the government camp for tourists, was able
to spend a great deal of his time taking us around to
the different cliff dwellings. I recall that we spent a
whole day in Cliff Palace, the cliff dwelling with a
tower, described in the *Tom Outland* part of *The
Professor's House,* cooking our lunch there and drinking
from the spring behind the cliff houses.

The day before we were to go back to Mancos,
Jeep had planned to take us to a cliff dwelling called
the Tower House, which had not then been exca-
vated. But just as we were about to start on this excursion, a large party of tourists arrived, and Jeep
announced that he would not be able to go with us.
He said that, instead, he would send us with his
brother-in-law, a young man named Richnor. We were
disappointed, for Jeep was a splendid guide, familiar
with every foot of the Mesa, and we knew nothing
about Richnor. However, as Jeep made this announce-

ment in Richnor's presence, we could hardly decline, and we started off with him.

To get to the Tower House, one had to walk through the woods to the rim of Soda Canyon, climb down to the bottom of this canyon, and follow along it for some distance. The Tower House was up the other wall of the canyon.

Richnor got us to the Tower House all right, but by a very rough trail—in climbing down to the bottom of Soda Canyon, we had in many places to hang from a tree or rock and then drop several feet to the next rock; we could not have returned by this trail without ropes. Richnor said he would take us back by another trail, further down the canyon. But by five or six o'clock that evening, after we had done a good many miles of walking, he was still unable to find this trail, and had to admit that he did not know how we were to get back. (The sides of the canyon were everywhere precipitous, and for several hundred feet beneath the rim the bare rock generally overhung.)

We had by then come to a place where another canyon, Cliff Canyon, opened at right angles from Soda Canyon. Richnor told us he thought, but was not sure, that about four miles up Cliff Canyon there was an archaeologist's camp (Dr. Fewkes' camp), and suggested that we try for it. But Willa Cather sensibly told him

he had better go up Cliff Canyon and find out whether
the camp was really there; we would wait, in the meantime, at the intersection of the two canyons.

The four or five hours that we spent waiting there
were, I think, for Willa Cather the most rewarding
of our whole trip to the Mesa Verde. There was a
large flat rock at the mouth of Cliff Canyon, and we
settled ourselves comfortably on this rock—with the
idea, I believe, that we should be able to see any rattlesnakes if they came racing up. We were tired and rather
thirsty, but not worried, for we knew we should eventually be found. We did not talk, but watched the long
summer twilight come on, and the full moon rise up
over the rim of the canyon. The place was very beautiful.

We were sitting there in the moonlight, when we
heard shouts from up Cliff Canyon, and presently two
men came in sight. They were two of the diggers from
Dr. Fewkes' camp, whom Richnor had sent down to
get us. He himself was so exhausted by the time he
reached the camp that he was unable to come back.

Soda Canyon has a wide, grassy bottom—one simply walks along it—but Cliff Canyon is a very difficult canyon to climb—just a mass of broken rocks
all the way, some of them as big as a house. We could
never have got through without the help of the two

diggers, who were both splendid men—kind, chivalrous, resourceful, and full of high spirits and encouragement. They said there was nothing they enjoyed so much as spending the night in this way. Their names were Clint Scarf and Audrey Grey Pearl. Each of them took one of us by the hand and steadied us over the rocks. (At one place we had to lie down and be pulled through a sort of tunnel in the rocks.) Occasionally we would stop for a short time to rest, and then the men would quickly build a little fire, for an icy wind swept down the canyon at night. At one point the sole of my climbing boot ripped away from toe to heel; but Clint Scarf produced a rawhide thong from his trousers' pocket, made holes with his pocket-knife, and laced the shoe together again so skilfully that it gave me no more trouble.

About four miles up the canyon one could reach the top of the cliffs by mounting part way on the lopped-off branches of a huge pine tree, which was laid along the side of the cliff like a ladder. We got to Fewkes' camp at about two in the morning. Our two diggers then went out into the pasture, caught a couple of horses, hitched them to a wagon, and drove us back to our own camp. At eight o'clock that same morning our team and driver arrived to take us back to Mancos.

On the whole, we had greatly enjoyed this adventure. We suffered no ill effects from it, beyond feeling rather tired and stiff for a day or two. But much to Willa Cather's annoyance, an enterprising reporter heard of it, and telegraphed a New York paper that she had been "rescued" on the Mesa Verde, and *McClure's Magazine* sent her a whole bunch of clippings with this notice.

This was Willa Cather's only visit to the Mesa Verde. Not long afterward she wrote an article about the Mesa and the cliff dwellings for an Omaha newspaper. But it was not until the Fall of 1923, eight years afterward, that she wrote *The Professor's House*—of which the Mesa Verde was the real genesis.

From the Mesa Verde we went on to Taos, New Mexico, then little visited and very isolated—one had to drive a long way by team to get there, over a rough road. There was no artist colony in Taos then, though one or two painters lived there quietly; and no American hotel or boardinghouse. We stayed at a rather primitive but comfortable adobe hotel run by a Mexican woman.

We spent perhaps a month in Taos, riding about on horses which we rented from a Mexican at the rate of fifty cents a morning, or taking long drives with a team of horses which we drove ourselves. One saw the country much better in this way than from an automobile, was able to note all the contours of the land, all the detail; the streams, flowers, trees, rocks, and any traces of human habitation. It was necessary to be on the alert for every landmark, otherwise we were likely to lose our way on those long drives and horseback rides through unknown country. Each Mexican village had its own vivid identity and setting, did not look like all the other Mexican villages. Each little church had its special character, its own treasures.

This was Willa Cather's first stay in New Mexico, though she had stopped over at Santa Fé and Lamy on her journey to Arizona. The following summer we went back to Taos for a longer time; and this summer we visited Santa Fé, and explored the Española valley, and drove to Santa Cruz, where we called on that fine Belgian priest, Father Haltermann, of whom Willa Cather speaks in her letter to *The Commonweal* telling how she came to write *Death Comes for the Archbishop.*

It was not a tourist country then. The distances were too great, the roads too rough, to get about easily by team. There were few hotels—and except for the wonderful Harvey Houses, set like jewels along the Santa Fé railroad, the ones there were were very primitive; they existed chiefly for the use of travelling salesmen. It was difficult to get any information about places not

on the beaten track; one picked it up here and there
from drivers, railroad men, an occasional Indian trader.
Willa Cather had a great talent for this sort of discovery; a name, a sentence let drop would start her off on
some ambitious new exploration.

She was intensely alive to the country—as a musician might be alive to an orchestral composition he
was hearing for the first time. She did not talk about
it much—but one felt that she was deeply engaged
with it always, was continually receiving strong impressions from the things she saw and experienced.

She loved the Southwest for its own sake. She did
not go there with any express purpose of writing about
it—of "gathering material," as they say, for a story.
She did not keep any notebook or diary; and so far
as I know, she did not write a line about it, save in
letters, during those early visits. She never spoke of
its literary possibilities. She was passionately interested in the country itself, in all its natural aspects—
and in the people, especially the Mexicans, and their
ways. It was in one of those first summers in Taos
that we drove with a team to Arroyo Hondo, and I
recall her excitement over the place, and its dramatic
approach. Long afterward her memory of it became
a part of the *Archbishop*. In the same way, once when
we were riding horseback in the sand desert west of

Taos, we were overtaken by a sudden hailstorm, and took refuge in a Mexican hut. Her impression of that interior, and the woman there, must have recurred to her when she wrote the chapter called *The Lonely Road to Mora*. Slight, vivid incidents like these stayed in her mind for years, to be drawn on when they were needed.

Willa Cather stopped in Red Cloud both of these summers, on her way back from the Southwest, while I went on to New York. When she returned to New York from the second trip, in the Fall of 1916, she brought with her the first two or three chapters of *My Ántonia*.

8 | "My Ántonia"

THAT winter and the following spring, Willa Cather worked without interruption on *My Ántonia*. Her friend Isabelle McClung, in the meantime, had married the violinist, Jan Hambourg; and in the early summer of 1917 the Hambourgs spent a few weeks at the Shattuck Inn, in Jaffrey, New Hampshire. They wrote to Willa Cather, urging her to join them there.

Aside from a few short excursions on Cape Ann, while she was living in Boston, this was Willa Cather's first experience of New England country. She took two small rooms on the top floor of the Shattuck Inn, and these rooms she always occupied when she went back to Jaffrey in later years. They had sloping ceilings, like her attic room in the old days in Red Cloud, and on the roof directly overhead she could hear the rain in wet weather. Her windows looked out over woods and juniper pastures toward Mount Monadnock, with its very individual outline.

A bellboy occupied the room next hers, and he was told by the management that he must be very quiet.

Indeed, few guests, probably, were ever more cherished and protected than was Willa Cather, both by the Shattucks, and later by their daughter and her husband, the Austermanns, who afterward ran the Shattuck Inn. The fact that she was a celebrity meant, I think, little to them; they were too much New Englanders for that. They had a great admiration and liking for her character.

That first summer the Inn was crowded with guests, and to give her greater quiet and seclusion two Pittsburgh friends, Miss Lucy Hine and Miss Acheson, who rented a place called *High Mowing* not far from the Shattuck Inn, had the idea of putting up a tent in their meadow-land for Willa Cather to work in.

This turned out an ideal arrangement. The tent was about half a mile from the Inn, by an unused wood road, and across a pasture or two. Willa Cather loved this solitary half-mile walk through the woods, and found it the best possible prelude to a morning of work. She wrote for two or three hours every day, surrounded by complete silence and peace. In the afternoons she took long walks about the countryside and up Monadnock mountain, often carrying with her Mathews' *Field Book of American Flowers,* her favourite botany.

Of all the places Willa Cather knew and enjoyed during her life—and places, different kinds of country, were rather a dominant note in her scale of enjoyment—Jaffrey became the one she found best to work in. The fresh, pine-scented woods and pastures, with their multitudinous wild flowers, the gentle skies, the little enclosed fields, had in them nothing of the disturbing, exalting, impelling memories and associations of the past—her own past. Each day there was like an empty canvas, a clean sheet of paper to be filled. She lived with a simple sense of physical well-being, of weather, and of country solitude.

For many years after that first summer Willa Cather spent her autumns in Jaffrey—going there about the middle of September and staying often late into November. Autumn was the most propitious season—the heat and the mosquitoes were gone then, the summer crowds had left, and there is nothing lovelier in the world than the New England Fall. When we later built a cottage on the island of Grand Manan in the Bay of Fundy, and went there for many of our summers, Willa Cather generally stopped for a month or so in Jaffrey on her way back, before returning to New York.

We read the proofs of *My Ántonia* together in Jaffrey early the following summer. Willa Cather liked to read proofs out of doors whenever it was possible; and one could always find convenient rocks to sit against in the woods near the Shattuck Inn. Those were wonderful mornings, full of beauty and pleasure. I remember how the chipmunks used to flash up and down along the trunks of the trees as we worked, and a mole would steal out of its hole near us and slide like a dark shadow along the ground. The air seemed full of the future—a future of bright prospects, limitless horizons.

It was very interesting to read proofs with Willa Cather. After a thing was written, she had an extremely impersonal attitude toward it. If there was "too much" of anything, she was not only ready, she was eager to cut it. She did not cherish her words and phrases. Sometimes she would have a sudden illumination and would make some radical change—always, I think, for the better. She had to pay nearly $150 for extra proof corrections on *My Ántonia*. Afterwards she was more provident, and made most of her changes in the typewritten copies of her manuscripts.

Houghton Mifflin published the book that Fall. Although Ferris Greenslet wrote a highly favourable report on it to the publishers, Willa Cather was disappointed, and I think rather disheartened, by their reception of the story. She herself felt that it was the best thing she had done—that she had succeeded, more nearly than ever before, in writing the way she wanted to write.

It is hard, now, to realize how revolutionary in form *My Ántonia* was at that time in America. It seemed to many people to have no form. It had no love story—though the whole book was a sort of love story of the country. *The Virginian* was the popular type of Western novel. Even Mrs. Fields, so personally devoted to Willa Cather, rather deplored the book—because it was about "hired girls". She preferred reading about the sort of people she found in Henry James' and Mrs. Humphrey Ward's novels. Her "dear Mr. Dickens", although he wrote of low life, always had gentlefolk for his heroes and heroines.

Most of the press notices praised the book highly—though a critic writing for the *New York Herald* of October 6, 1918 said:—

"I regret to see a writer of such fine literary quality as Miss Willa S. Cather seek expression through those dreary channels that traverse life on the Western prairies like so many irrigation ditches . . . As a novel, it will prove a disappointment to everyone who has read Miss Cather's earlier work."

On the other hand H. L. Mencken—from the beginning one of Willa Cather's warmest champions—wrote:—

"*My Ántonia* is not only the best novel done by Miss Cather, but also one of the best any American has ever done."

The initial sale of *My Ántonia* was small—in the first year it brought Willa Cather about $1,300, and not quite $400 the second year. She had begun to feel that she could never write the kind of book that would be wholly satisfactory to Houghton Mifflin as publishers. Yet she had confidence in what she was doing, and the reception of her books among people whose opinion she respected had increased that confidence. What action she took next can best be told in her own account of her first meeting with Alfred Knopf, written for a little volume—*Alfred A. Knopf: Quarter Century*—contributed by his friends on his 25th anniversary as publisher. She called it *Portrait of the Publisher as a Young Man.**

"I first went to Alfred Knopf," she wrote, "in the early spring of 1920. I went in a very literal sense— going by the West Side subway to his office in the Candler Building on West 42nd Street. On the nineteenth floor I found his place of business: a large, un-

*Copyright 1940 by Alfred A. Knopf, Inc.

furnished floor space, with a small office partitioned
off at one corner. In this corner the publisher sat at
his desk. In the big room outside, two or three young
lads were working in their shirt sleeves, apparently
tying up parcels of books. This seemed to be all
there was to the new publishing house.

"I had never met Mr. Knopf, and he had never
made a gesture in my direction. But from the time he
published Hudson's *Green Mansions*, (1916) I had
watched his venture with keen interest. He seemed to
be doing something new, and doing it with conviction.
I remembered a short pamphlet on Joseph Conrad,
sent out by the Doubleday house, but signed Alfred A.
Knopf. That must have been back in 1912 or '13.
I remembered the pamphlet because it expressed a
sincere enthusiasm and was not at all like the usual
'personality publicity.' When I saw the name 'Knopf'
on the jacket of *Green Mansions*, I thought at once
that this must be the same young man.

"I liked the look of those early Borzoi books. Every
publisher nowadays tries to make his books look interesting (jacket, cover, type, make-up), but in so far
as my knowledge goes it was Alfred Knopf who set
the fashion. His early books looked very different
from other books that came out at the same time. I
was convinced that he had set out to do something

unusual and individual in publishing. That was why
I went uninvited to call on him.

"Our conversation that morning was entirely impersonal. Neither of us indulged in any flattery. We
talked about some books we liked very much, and
some we didn't like. I asked him what was the first
book he had published. He said a good translation of
some of Emile Augier's plays; he had to take what he
could get. When I picked up some samples of blue
binding paper which lay on his desk, he told me he
intended to use that material for a book of Chinese
poems translated by Arthur Waley. He had gone to
the Metropolitan Museum of Art to find exactly the
right shade from among the Chinese blues. 'We
haven't much money to spend here,' he added, 'but
we'll take any amount of pains with a book.' This
was not said with any savor of self-satisfaction, or in
the 'We-do-our-best' manner. On the contrary it was
flung out in a distinctly challenging tone,—as if I,
or somebody else, did not take much pains.

"In the course of our talk I discovered that the
young man felt a strong loyalty for some of his professors at Columbia University, and that he admired
several English writers who were taken for granted
over here, but little read. He seemed to have more degrees and shades of color in both his likings and his

scorn than most people have. And he seemed to be going into this business as if it were an exhilarating sport of some kind. His talk was amazingly free and human. No timidity, no evasions, no string of qualifying phrases ('weasel words'). The gates of the donjon hadn't closed on him at all—I didn't believe they ever would. And, with all his rashness and his challenging air, what was he actually putting his money on? Not on the shilling shocker or the devilish boys; but on old Mr. Hudson, revered but not read; on Augier, whose plays French fathers used to take their children to see.—A fiery temperament and a rather severe taste; such a combination is possible in a collector . . . but in a publisher?

"Something interesting would go on here, of that I felt sure, and I wanted, in some capacity or other, to be in on it. Before I left the office that morning I asked the young man if he would consider becoming my publisher. He said he thought we would better both consider; changing publishers was a serious matter, after all.

"At our second meeting a few days later, Mr. Knopf said he thought we might try it out together, if I had anything ready to publish. I was just then in the middle of a long book, and had nothing to offer him but a collection of short stories, five of which had been published before. A few months later he put them out in a volume entitled *Youth and the Bright Medusa.*

"In the detail work of getting out a book a publisher and a writer find out a good deal about each other. Mr. Knopf and I soon found that we had several predilections and several prejudices in common; they helped to establish a personal relationship.

"Through the next five years his list grew amazingly, and he introduced a number of the best European writers to this country. Among the finest books he put out were many which could not possibly yield him a quick financial return. He published them because they were fine books, by writers of proved authority, or by fresh talent—which he was quick to recognize. The appearance of Thomas Mann (in a remarkably fine translation), of Sigrid Undset and Knut Hamsun, meant a great deal to the American reading public and to young American writers. All of Katherine Mansfield's stories were published, in this country, under the Borzoi imprint.

"There have been many elements in Mr. Knopf's success, but I think the most important and characteristic are his quick and sharp reactions: to a manuscript, to a business proposition, to an individual. He knows at once what books he likes, and what people he likes. He has, of course, published books he thought very second-rate, and he has successfully done business with people who were not congenial to him. But in his own mind he kept the two sets of values apart, clear and distinct. He never tried to persuade himself that a book he had found quite commonplace must, after all, have some remarkable merit merely because he sold a great many copies. He has always had a good word for painstaking, honest work, however uninspired, and for blundering beginners. But when a book takes hold of him, whether it is put out by his own house or by another publisher, I know it in a moment by something in his voice and in his eye. He can consider a manuscript leniently as a publishing proposition, and do full justice to it. But when he really likes a book, he likes it with a keenness and freshness which must be a great help to any writer. I often wonder how anyone who has read so many manuscripts can keep that fresh appetite for live writing which Alfred and Blanche Knopf still have. There are two Knopfs, one must remember; and certainly Alfred could never have done his work alone. Very often Mr. Knopf has to be on one side of the Atlantic and his wife on the other; an energetic publishing business must be both at home and abroad. Writers and agents on both sides of the water want to deal with *the House*, not with a representative employed by the house.

"When Alfred Knopf began his business in a two-room office for which he paid a rental of forty-five dollars a month, he was a free agent; he had nobody's money to lose but his own, and very little of that, as he frankly told me. He seemed then a daring and reckless figure flashing into a company of grave and experienced competitors. Twenty years ago 'caution' was the watchword in all reputable publishing houses, just as 'abandon' is the slogan today. Yet Mr. Knopf's daring experiment was soon repeated by other young men who went beyond him in daring. He is now generally regarded as a conservative. He still prefers good writing when he can get it, has a liking for clear syntax, and does not publish the tough girl or the crook for the sole reason that they are tough and crooked. He has a respect for the English language as it was used by the great masters of the past, and for the American language which is being joyously made and remade all the time by every wide-awake office boy and truck driver between the two oceans. He seems to believe that these two languages, the one or the other, or the two skillfully blended, can hold all the intelligence, all the feeling and fun, that any writer can put into them. But in some trifles he is severely conventional; if he has published any books with no commas or periods, I haven't seen them. He has no objection to using an upper-case letter at the beginning of a line of verse. Although from the first he has been conspicuous for his interest in types and make-up, assaults upon punctuation and the upper-case have left him cold.

"It has been interesting to watch a business grow into a strong house, recognized at home and abroad, without at all losing that individual quality it had from the beginning. In his professional conferences Alfred Knopf may be mild and non-committal, as business men are supposed to be. But about books and music he is as fierce as ever. There he has never learned to soft-pedal very successfully; we hope he never will.

"I have always been proud that I asked young Mr. Knopf to take me over, with not so much as a hint from him that he would like to have me. It was a rather sudden decision. Did it work? The answer is, twenty years."

Next to writing her novels, Willa Cather's choice of Alfred Knopf as a publisher influenced her career, I think, more than any action she ever took. It was not so much that with him she was able in a few years to achieve financial security (in 1923, after the publication of her Pulitzer prize novel, *One of Ours*, the royalties on her two Knopf books alone—*One of Ours* and *Youth and the Bright Medusa*—were over $19,000), as that he gave her great encouragement and absolute liberty to write exactly as she chose—protected her in every way he could from outside pressures and interruptions —and made evident, not only to her but to the world in general, his great admiration and belief in her. Life was simply no longer a battle—she no longer had to feel apologetic or on the defensive. She was always very modest about her work, but she was a person of great pride. Her pride was no longer threatened.

9 "One of Ours"

THE "long book" Willa Cather was in the middle of, when she had her first interview with Alfred Knopf, was *One of Ours*.

She was the last person to have set out deliberately to write a "war novel." She felt strongly about the war from its beginning, for it threatened everything in the world of the mind's endeavour that was most precious to her; she saw it beforehand, I think, as many people saw it afterward. But she talked very little about it, and it would not, I am sure, have occurred to her to write about it except for an accident.

It was the news, in May, 1918, of a favourite cousin's death at the head of his men in the battle of Cantigny—the first American offensive—that gave her the idea of writing *One of Ours*.

He was a Nebraska boy, and she had known him from childhood. There had been a strong feeling of kinship and sympathy between them. That summer, after *Ántonia* was finished, she went out to Nebraska again. It was one of the great harvest years—and Nebraska can be very thrilling in the harvest season. She was in an extremely impressionable state of mind, and everything she saw and experienced must have fed her idea of the story she wanted to write.

After she got back to New York, she began seeing and talking with a great many soldiers. A former devoted high school pupil, Albert Donovan, had an army post in New York which brought him into contact with numbers of enlisted men; and when he learned that Willa Cather was writing a story that had to do with the war, he used to bring them, three and four at a time, to 5 Bank Street. They would stay for hours talking to Willa Cather.

She worked on *One of Ours* all through 1919. Late in the summer she went back to Jaffrey, where she again had her tent. It was a very rainy season, and writing in her tent in the rain, she got a severe attack of influenza. The local doctor attended her; and in one of his visits she learned that he had served as a medical officer on a troop ship of the A. E. F. during a very bad influenza epidemic which broke out on board; and that he had kept a diary all through the voyage.

He let Willa Cather borrow this diary; and it was from this that she wrote the part of *One of Ours* called *The Voyage of the Anchises*.

(He later told her an amusing incident that happened to him:—He was relating one of his experiences during this epidemic to a friend, and the friend said coldly: "That isn't a true story. You took that from Willa Cather's book!")

In the spring of 1920 Willa Cather had completed two-thirds of *One of Ours;* but to write the remaining third she felt she must spend some time in France. I got a long leave of absence from my office job, and in June, 1920, we took passage on an old liner, *The Royal George,* landing at Cherbourg. We went to Paris, and lived for the next six or seven weeks at the *Hotel du Quai Voltaire,* on the left bank of the Seine.

Though friends had given Willa Cather introductions to a number of people in Paris they wanted her to meet, she did not use any of them. She said she wanted to live in the Middle Ages. And we did live in the Middle Ages, so far as it was possible. We hardly ever went beyond the Tuilleries on the right bank of the Seine, except to get money, and occasionally to hear opera at the *Opéra-Comique.* We spent nearly all our time in the section between the Seine and the Luxembourg gardens, and on the Île de la Cité and the Île-St. Louis.

Willa Cather had a great gift for imaginative historical reconstruction. There was nothing of the antiquarian in her; she did not care for old things because they were old or curious or rare—she cared for them only as they expressed the human spirit and the human lot on earth. She had an almost magical gift of interpreting their language. She could make the modern age almost disappear, fade away and become ghostlike, so completely was she able to invoke her vision of the past and recreate its reality.

Many years afterward, when we went to Virginia together, I saw this happen again. It was as if she were able to turn back the visible landscape, with its gas stations, hot dog stands, macadam roads, and advertising signs, as one might turn back a rug; and underneath it one saw the living pattern of another civilization and way of life. It was not only her talk that did this; it was the fact that she herself went back and lived this life and refused to come out of it. It became for the time being her life.

The Middle Ages may not seem to have had much to do with the story she was then writing; but in a way they did. She had to get the feeling of the whole of France to write about it.

At the end of seven weeks or so, her friends the Hambourgs arrived in Paris—Jan Hambourg had offered to go with her to the battlefields and steer her about there. He was a very good French scholar, and skilful about arranging all the details of travel. While I went to Italy to visit friends, she and the Hambourgs travelled for a couple of weeks in the devastated part of France. She found her cousin's grave, and wrote a long letter to his mother about it. In late August we rejoined one another in the south of France and journeyed slowly back to Paris, where we stayed at the *Quai Voltaire* until late October. She had become restless, and wanted to get home to work, and I believe it was only because I pleaded to stay on a while longer that she put off her return as long as she did.

One of Ours was published in September, 1922, and became the subject of a good deal of controversy. Dos Passos' *Three Soldiers* had been published a short time before; and Sinclair Lewis' *Babbitt* came out almost simultaneously with *One of Ours*; the two were sometimes reviewed together. Sinclair Lewis was asked to write a criticism of Willa Cather's novel for the *Literary Review* of the New York *Evening Post*. In the course of his review he said: "The whole introduction of the great war is doubtful; it is a matter to be debated." Willa Cather had not, of course, "introduced" the war in the sense in which Lewis wrote; it was an intrinsic part of her original conception. I think she never changed the fundamental design of a book, except in the case of *O Pioneers!*. In all her other novels the idea came to her as a whole, the end as well as the beginning, and writing the novel was simply an attempt to realize her first vision of it. In *One of Ours* she did not choose the war as a theme, and then set out to interpret it through the experience of one individual. The whole story was born from a personal experience (as I think was the case with all her novels); from the way in which the news of her cousin's death at Cantigny brought suddenly before her an intense realization of his nature and his life, and their significance. To her he was not, as Sinclair Lewis wrote, "so heroic, so pure, so clever, so noble, that no one could believe in him." He was a boy she had known well, and she wrote of him as she knew him. Moreover, he did not seem to her exceptional, except in the way that every individual is exceptional; she felt that she had known many American boys like *Claude*.

Although he did not care for *One of Ours*, Lewis was in general one of Willa Cather's most generous admirers. When he was given the Nobel Prize, he declared publicly that she was the one who should have had it; and wrote her that he would gladly give nine Nobel prizes to have written *Death Comes for the Archbishop*.

The letters she got from soldiers about the book pleased her more than anything else she got from it.

"I was in France for over three years, first with the French Foreign Legion, and later with the Americans. And I think that the last part of *One of Ours* is the most perfect picture of the war that I have read."—"I am twenty-two myself, Miss Cather, and you have created me in Claude."—"I cannot express the emotions you have aroused—I have not felt them since I went through Hoboken in a troop train."—this was the sort of thing they wrote. Some of the letters might have been written by *Claude Wheeler* himself.

One of Ours was given the Pulitzer Prize award—it was the first of her books to have a popular success. The spring before it was published, Willa Cather had already begun *A Lost Lady*.

"A Lost Lady"

ALTHOUGH *A Lost Lady* has been regarded by many critics as the most perfect in form of all her novels, Willa Cather had, at the start, more trouble with it than with any of the others. As a rule she was unhesitating in her attack on a new piece of work. She did not try first one way and then another, but took at once, with sureness and great momentum, the road she wished to follow. Her difficulty in the case of *A Lost Lady* arose largely, I think, from the fact that *Mrs. Forrester* was more a direct portrait than any of her other characters except *Ántonia*; and although Mrs. Garber, from whom *Mrs. Forrester* was drawn, and her husband, Governor Garber, were both dead, some of their relatives were alive and might be (and, indeed, were) offended. Probably because of this, she at first set the scene of her story in Colorado, and wrote it at some length in this setting. But she found it would not work. Her memories of Mrs. Garber, and of the Garber place, were among the strongest, most enduring impressions of her childhood; a whole ambiance of thought and feeling surrounded them, and she could not transfer them to an artificial climate. So she started the story anew, writing of things just as she remembered them.

But she still was not wholly satisfied with the construction of the story. As nearly as I can recall, her dissatisfaction arose from the difficulty of maintaining what she felt to be the right balance in the presentation, which is sometimes direct, but more often done through the boy *Niel*. When she had written perhaps one-third of the story, she decided to change and write it all in the first person, and she recommenced it a second time, and wrote several chapters in this manner.

That June she had accepted an invitation to give two or three talks before the English classes at Breadloaf, Vermont, where a school for advanced students was held every summer. She took the two versions of *A Lost Lady*, so far as she had written them, along with her, and in the week or so that she spent at Breadloaf she went over them; and came then to the conclusion that her first method was right. She discarded the chapters she had written in the first person, and from that time on wrote the story without any break or hesitation.

Perhaps at this point I might say something about Willa Cather's method of working. When she began a novel, she began it, I think, somewhat as one might undertake a journey. She knew her direction and her destination, and some of the places she might visit on the way; but she never carefully plotted out beforehand the actual journey itself—the scenes and incidents and surprises, the changes and complications. I think this would have spoiled all her pleasure in writing. And to her, writing was an intense and, I believe, an unmixed pleasure. She never wrote laboriously, never had to struggle for expression. Writing with her was a form of improvisation, controlled and guided, of course, by a firm underlying design. She often said that when she sat down at her desk, she did not in the least know what she was going to write. This did not mean, of course, that she did not know where she was going. She depended on the force of her idea and her feeling to create the pattern of her story as she went along, and it was this activity of creating the thing as she wrote that she enjoyed—enjoyed with a sense of exhilaration, as one might enjoy a fast game of tennis. She always wrote her first draft with great speed—not stopping to change a word or a phrase, intent only on capturing the rapid flow of her ideas. She generally worked from two to three hours in the morning, and did not touch her work again that day. The following day she would continue from where she had left off— not going back over what she had written until the whole thing was completed.

Although she did not plan the actual content of a novel beforehand, I believe one could say that she lived a great deal with her idea (though she rarely talked about her mental processes; she disliked any form of self-analysis). During the time she was not writing, or engaged with something else, I think she was very much preoccupied with the past out of which her story sprang; not actively trying to construct anything, but surrendering herself to memories, impressions, experiences, that lay submerged in her consciousness; letting them come to the surface, and relate themselves to the theme of her narrative.

When she had written the first draft of her story by hand, she rewrote the whole thing on her typewriter, keeping the hand-written version beside her, but not always following it—she would sometimes write several pages quite differently, would add things that were not in the first draft, or omit parts altogether. This type-written version she would then give to her secretary to copy. She generally had it re-copied more than once, making corrections and changes each time, and she also corrected and revised carefully all the proofs.

It was while she was writing *A Lost Lady* that Willa Cather first began to work at Grand Manan. That summer we rented a little cottage called *Orchardside* from Miss Sarah Jacobus, who ran a small place for summer guests at Whale Cove on Grand Manan.

Grand Manan is an island about twenty miles long and seven or eight miles wide, lying at the mouth of the Bay of Fundy. Most of the island is wooded, and around the greater part are cliffs from two to four hundred feet high; but on one side the land slopes down to the sea, and along this side are four or five little fishing villages. Herring fishing is the chief industry of the place.

Living conditions were, of course, rather primitive on Grand Manan. Mail, and most supplies, were brought from the mainland (a trip of five or six hours) on a small steamboat which sailed twice a week from St. John, New Brunswick, Canada's chief winter port. The little cottage Willa Cather and I rented had been built more than a hundred years before, by a cooper who lived on the Island. There was no plumbing, one had a washbowl and pitcher for washing purposes, and drafts came in on every side through the cracks of the floor and window-frames—on windy nights the rug in the living-room would ripple in waves along the floor. But wood was cheap and plentiful, and in the evenings, and whenever the weather was damp or chilly, we kept fires of white birch logs going in the large brick fireplace.

The outdoor surroundings were unsurpassably lovely. The weather had a perpetual enchantment; it was always changing, and all the changes were interesting and beautiful. There was a kind of gentleness and innocence in the natural character of the Island; wild flowers grew everywhere in the clean grass, the streams that rushed in waterfalls over the cliffs were pure and uncontaminated, the wild creatures that lived in the woods never harmed anybody; even the slender, emerald-green snakes one occasionally met on the paths seemed friendly and sociable—did not glide away as one approached. The wild snow-shoe hares that came close to the cottage to nibble at the clover would creep under the very chair one was sitting in. Birds often built their nests four or five feet from the ground in the little spruce trees. Sometimes, at dawn or dusk, one encountered a deer or fawn.

There was solitude without loneliness. One could walk for miles along the cliffs without meeting anyone or seeing any mark of human life; but there was always activity on the water. Small craft of all kinds went to and fro, setting out lines, visiting the herring weirs, carrying lumber. Indians from the reservation at Point Pleasant sometimes paddled over to the Island in their canoes—looking down from the cliffs one would see a string of them rounding a point.

Although there were a good many physical discomforts to put up with, the quiet, the great remove from all mundane things, and the natural loveliness of the place made Grand Manan, in the summer, a better place to work than any other Willa Cather had found. The climate was delightful—warm, bright days and cool nights. It rained a good deal, but rainy weather there had an extreme beauty and interest—was not something negative and disappointing.

It was in the summer of 1925, three years later, that we decided to build a small cottage on Grand Manan. Willa Cather felt that it would be an advantage to have a sort of summer camp where she could come and go at will—where she would not have to make arrangements in advance, keep set dates, etc.—and where she could live with complete independence. A builder on the Island built the cottage in our absence, during the Fall and Spring, after one of us had staked it out beforehand. It stood on a sloping hillside, about fifty yards from the edge of the cliffs, in the middle of an open meadow, and was surrounded by a semicircle of spruce and birch woods. It was rather a rough little place, with many inconveniences; but it came to have not only comfort, but great charm. Above the living rooms was a large attic from which one could look out over the cliffs and the sea, and this Willa Cather chose for her study. There was nothing in it except a few trunks, and her chair and table.

A Lost Lady was completed in the Spring of 1923. That summer Willa Cather went again to France, to visit the Hambourgs, who had bought a house at Ville d'Avray near Paris, and had written repeatedly begging her to come and stay with them. They had arranged a little study in their house for her to work in; in fact they had hoped she would make Ville d'Avray her permanent home. But although the little study was charming, and all the surroundings were attractive, and the Hambourgs themselves devoted and solicitous, she found herself unable to work at Ville d'Avray. She felt, indeed, that she would never be able to do any work there.

The Public Library at Omaha, Nebraska, had written to Willa Cather that Spring or Summer, to say that they wished to have her portrait to hang in the Library, and had subscribed a sum of money for this purpose. They asked her to choose an artist to paint the portrait. Leon Bakst, then one of the great names in the world of art, was living in Paris, and friends strongly advised Willa Cather to arrange with him, if possible, to undertake the commission; and this she did. She had, I think, as many as twenty sittings with Bakst. His charm and genius, his winning, attractive personality made these sittings a delight, and the two became warm friends. But the portrait was a complete failure. It was not, of course, at all Bakst's kind of thing—and she felt that he would probably have resigned the commission when he saw how it was turning out, were it not for the fact that he was supporting half-a-dozen fellow-Russians in Paris at the time, and needed the money. As it was, he went on painting desperately at the portrait, sitting after sitting, while all the while it grew worse—stiff, dark, heavy, lifeless—everything that Willa Cather was not, and, indeed, everything that Bakst was not.

The Omaha Library people behaved most chivalrously about it; it was unveiled and hung with appropriate ceremonies, and no word of complaint or reproach ever came to Willa Cather from them, although they must have been deeply disappointed.

One incident during these sittings Willa Cather spoke of afterward: Nijinski was brought to Bakst's studio by a friend. He was quiet, gentle, extremely courteous; but after he had been introduced and had kissed her hand, he went, after a little, and stood in a corner of the studio with his face to the wall. He believed himself to be a horse.

After her sittings with Bakst were completed, Willa Cather went to Aix-les-Bains for several weeks, before returning to America. She did no work there, but it was perhaps in the peace and beauty of the Savoie countryside that the idea of *The Professor's House* took shape in her mind. She became very much attached to the little town itself, and resolved to go back there.

She returned to New York late in the Fall, and began at once to write *The Professor's House* at 5 Bank Street.

11 "The Professor's House" and "Death Comes for the Archbishop"

FOR a number of years, while she lived at 5 Bank Street, Willa Cather was at home to her friends every Friday afternoon. These Friday afternoons became very popular—so popular, in fact, that eventually she had to give them up; instead of half-a-dozen or so of her friends dropping in for tea, more and more people came, sometimes bringing strangers with them; and it became at last too much of a responsibility. But those informal gatherings around the coal fire in the living-room at 5 Bank Street, with the late winter sunlight slowly changing into dusk, and the melodious sound of the tugboat whistles coming up from the river near by, were very pleasant while they lasted. Every one talked as if there were not nearly time enough for all they had to say. Often a small group of Willa Cather's more intimate friends would stay on after the others had drifted away, lingering until eight o'clock or later, and driving the cook, Josephine, to despair; and the talk was then always at its best.

134

I still remember how Viola Roseboro' would sometimes appear on those Friday afternoons, stand in the doorway regarding the company (she had a very dramatic presence), and say reproachfully to Willa Cather, "Ah, I hoped that I should find you alone!"

I speak of these Friday afternoons because in after years there grew up a legend of Willa Cather's inaccessibility and love of seclusion, of her living the life of a recluse. She was never a recluse by nature. She loved people, and had a warm, eager, impulsive interest in all kinds of people. Her response to them was never languid or half-hearted, never perfunctory or withdrawn. She had a gift for immediately creating a personal relationship of some kind with anyone she met—with the saleswoman who waited on her, or the porter who moved her trunk. It was something more than good manners, or even charm. Perhaps it was her instant recognition of their common humanity, of the fact that their claim on life was equal to her own. Humble, unlettered people, to whom her books would have meant nothing, felt her quality at once; felt in her a superior power to understand life, and their own lives.

It was the completeness of her response to people that made ordinary human contacts more taxing for her than for most. Even during the McClure days she found meeting and talking to a long procession of callers the most exhausting part of her job. As she became more widely known, as her books became celebrated, the demands on her time and strength of course greatly increased. The luxury she prized above all others was freedom; and she now found her freedom hampered at every turn. When she went to a concert, women she did not know would come up to her and ask her to sit in their box. Strangers would address her on the street. If she went for a walk in Central Park, she would be stopped and asked to autograph a book. She was, of course, continually pressed to give interviews, to give lectures, to join societies, to work for charities—all the clutter of irrelevant activities that obstruct the life of any artist who becomes famous. But the one thing needful for her, as for most artists, was solitude—solitude not only to work in, but to feel and think in. She had no uncertainty as to what, for her, were the real values, and was never in the least influenced or intimidated by other people's standards. The struggle to preserve the integrity of her life as an artist, its necessary detachment and freedom, cost her something—cost a considerable expenditure of nervous energy, for it meant a steady exertion of her will against the will of the public. But it was not disdain for the tributes people wished to pay her, or a feeling of superiority or indifference, that caused her to withdraw more and more from the world. It was self-preservation.

During most of 1924, Willa Cather was working on *The Professor's House*. In June of that year, the University of Michigan gave her an honorary degree. One of the Wright brothers took a degree at the same time, and I recall her interest in the talk they had together. When she was living in Pittsburgh, she had known a close friend of Langley, who had been present at that last tragic experiment which brought down on Langley such a storm of ridicule and failure. She had always found Langley's story moving and fascinating, and it was about Langley that she talked with Wright. I think even the slight stimulus of this meeting contributed in a sense to the story she was then doing— not by adding in any way to her material, but because it somehow heightened and coloured her mood. Directly after this commencement we went to Grand Manan, where she wrote the part of *The Professor's House* called *Tom Outland's Story*.

The Professor's House is, I think, the most personal of Willa Cather's novels—and for that cause, no doubt, is given a more symbolic expression than her other stories. It has always been a favourite with professors! William Lyon Phelps of Yale University, who ranked it highest among her works, called it "a terrifying novel." E. K. Brown, of Chicago University, gave it one of his subtlest and most profound interpretations in his essay, *Interweaving Themes** (first delivered as one of the Alexander lectures at the University of Toronto, and afterward published, with his other lectures of the series, in his fascinating book, *Rhythm in the Novel*).

Willa Cather's own letter on *The Professor's House*, which she permitted to be published in her life-time, and which is included in the volume *Willa Cather on Writing*, gives a clue to the story's unusual form; but as Stephen Tennant, in his Preface to that volume, has so sensitively recognized, form itself is here a kind of symbol; and his title, *The Room Beyond*, states imaginatively what in fact became more and more Willa Cather's preoccupation as an artist:—the bringing into being of something beyond the situation or the characters of a story, something beyond the story itself,—the unseen vision, the unheard echo, which attend all experience.

The following Spring Willa Cather wrote the short novel *My Mortal Enemy* at 5 Bank Street. It was this Spring that she came to know the D. H. Lawrences. They had spent the summer before in Ceylon, sharing a bungalow with friends of ours, Earl Brewster and his

*Much of this essay is now incorporated in his biography of Willa Cather.

beautiful wife, both very interesting painters; and the Brewsters had begged Lawrence to look us up while he and Frieda were in New York. They came two successive afternoons to 5 Bank Street, and Willa Cather found them very attractive—Lawrence especially so, for he was on these occasions in his sunniest mood, and his talk was very vivid and amusing. They did not speak at all of books—Lawrence talked chiefly of their life in Ceylon. He had a wonderful faculty for giving one the tastes, the smells, the colours and sounds of a place. He imitated, I remember, the sounds the leopards made, when they leaped on the roof of the bungalow at night, hunting for mice in the thatch; and told us about the snakes, for which a native with a gun was employed about the grounds, to keep constant watch. When they said goodbye, they spoke of our all meeting again in New Mexico.

Willa Cather had long wanted to return to the Southwest. It may be that the many impressions she gathered on her visits to that country had begun to suggest ideas for stories. But no definite design for a novel had formed itself in her mind until we went that summer (the summer of 1925) to New Mexico, stopping first in Santa Fé. There, in a single evening, as she often said, the idea of *Death Comes for the Archbishop* came to her, essentially as she afterwards wrote it.

From that time on it completely took possession of her, filled all her waking thoughts. She knew exactly what material she needed in order to write the story as she wanted to write it, and she seemed to draw it out of everything she encountered—from the people she talked with—old settlers, priests, taxi-drivers, Indian traders, trainmen; from old books she found in the various libraries in Santa Fé, and used to bring back to the hotel by the armful, and read in the evening; and from the country itself. We drove all over northern New Mexico, this time by automobile. She made notes occasionally about dates and facts she took from her reading; but I do not think she made any notes of things she herself encountered. She trusted to her memory to retain anything of real interest or importance.

I have forgotten whether it was that summer or the following summer that we went by train to Gallup, and from there drove through the striped pine forests of the Navajo country to the Cañon de Chelly. We had for our driver a fine young fellow named Allen— who some years later was driving Mrs. Harold Ickes, the wife of the Secretary of the Interior, along a canyon road, when his car plunged over the edge of the canyon, and they both were killed. I have always remembered Allen as one of the most attractive and intelligent and loyal of our drivers. But he seemed pursued by bad luck. That day, I recall, he lost his way in the midst of a vast plain encircled by great mesas, and was several hours finding it again. Then his car broke down, and for a while it looked as if we might have to spend the night there in the open. But it was precisely accidents like these that always heightened the special character of a journey, and fixed the light, the colours, the whole mood of one's surroundings forever in the memory. By changing the key of an experience, they sometimes became one of its most valuable elements.

On one of Willa Cather's returns to Santa Fé from her journeys about the country, Mabel Luhan called on her and asked her to visit her at her hacienda in Taos. With one or two exceptions, Willa Cather never visited anyone; and at this time especially she wanted to be absolutely free to follow her own devices. But Mabel Luhan was very persistent, in a quiet, persuasive way. She offered Willa Cather one of her guest houses to stay in—the Pink House, where the Lawrences had stayed—and promised that she should never be bothered by anyone, need never see anyone, except when she came over for meals; and Willa Cather finally agreed to come for two or three days.

Before going to Taos, we stopped for a week at the

Pfeffle Ranch, in the Española valley, between the Black Mesa and the desert, and read the proofs of *The Professor's House*.

Mabel Luhan arrived at the end of the week in her car, with Tony Luhan, the Taos Indian whom she had married, and they drove us to Taos. Willa Cather was very much impressed by Tony Luhan, and felt an instant liking and admiration for him. He was a splendid figure, over six feet tall, with a noble head and dignified carriage; there was great simplicity and kindness in his voice and manner. Although Willa Cather had intended to make a very brief visit, we stayed for more than two weeks. During that time Mabel Luhan, while making her guests extremely comfortable, rarely appeared herself, excepting at meals; but she sent us off on long drives about the country with Tony. Tony would sit in the driver's seat, in his silver bracelets and purple blanket, often singing softly to himself; while we sat behind. He took us to some of the almost inaccessible Mexican villages hidden in the Cimmaron mountains, where the Penitentes still followed their old fierce customs; and from Tony, Willa Cather learned many things about the country and the people that she could not have learned otherwise. He talked very little, but what he said was always illuminating and curiously poetic.

Although *Eusabio* in *Death Comes for the Archbishop* is a Navaho Indian, I think his character was essentially drawn from Tony Luhan.

While we were visiting Mabel Luhan, we went to call on the D. H. Lawrences, who were then living at the ranch Mrs. Luhan had given Lawrence, in return for the manuscript of *Sons and Lovers*. This ranch was up in the mountains about twenty-five miles from Taos. He and Frieda Lawrence were living very simply and even roughly; they baked their own bread, milked their own cow—Lawrence, I remember, had just been off hunting the cow over a four-square-mile pasture. His talk, as before, was full of charm and vivacity, sometimes with a satirical edge to it, but without any of the polemics which I believe sometimes characterized it. Nothing could have been friendlier or more hospitable than their welcome.

Her two visits to Mrs. Luhan—for she stayed with her a second time the following summer—were very rewarding to Willa Cather. Mabel Luhan—essentially an artist herself—knew the conditions that contribute to an artist's work, and was able to create them. She had, too, a large, ungrudging generosity toward people she admired; one felt that she enjoyed helping them toward their aim and seeing them realize their desires.

That Fall, after we got back from the Southwest, Willa Cather went straight to Jaffrey; and it was there that she wrote—at a sitting, as it seems to me now—the magnificent introduction to *Death Comes for the Archbishop*.

She worked all winter at 5 Bank Street, with unusual happiness and serenity. But as the actual writing of the story progressed, she found there were many things and places she must learn about, and many details she wanted to verify; so in July we set out again for New Mexico. On this trip we went for the first time to Ácoma. It was a curiously interesting and memorable experience.

At that time the Santa Fé trains stopped at Laguna, where the beautiful Laguna pueblo is. From there one had to hire a car to go to Ácoma, about thirty miles away. When we got off the train, there was no one to help us with our suitcases except two little girls, about eight and ten years old. They told us that "two ladies"—their mother and the cook—ran the hotel. The hotel turned out to be the roughest and dirtiest we had ever stopped in. The poor, overworked woman who kept it never had time to sweep it—there were great clods of earth on the carpets. The windowpanes in our bedrooms were broken in jagged holes, and burnt matches and cigarette papers were scattered all

over the floor. The only bathroom was down a flight
of stairs and at the end of a long, dark corridor. All
the food in the hotel came out of cans, including the
milk and butter.

Behind the hotel was a wretched "tourist's camp,"
where families in old cars crusted with mud, and with
mattresses tied to them, often stopped for the night.
Sometimes they would try to leave before dawn, so as
not to have to pay the 50 cents fee.

We had intended to stay in Laguna overnight, drive
to Ácoma, and go on the next day. But it turned out
to be a season of cloudbursts. Every day there were
heavy rains, and the road to Ácoma was impassable for
a car. We had to stay in Laguna a week.

Yet during that week, in those very uncomfortable
surroundings, Willa Cather often said afterwards she
got the most constructive ideas for her story that she
had in the whole course of writing it.

The hotel was almost empty. One guest I remember, a prosperous Mexican named Mr. Narcissus, who
arrived in Laguna with a flock of fifty prize rams, with
wonderful curling horns—each ram valued at $500.
The food at the hotel was so bad that we often bought
crackers and cheese at the Indian trader's, taking it out
to eat on the ledges behind the pueblo. A very interesting little French family kept the railway station—

the daughter was the railway telegrapher, and used to throw the messages to the engineers of the fast trains, as they ran through without stopping. It was pleasant to sit on the bench outside the station house and watch the life that came and went. The Laguna Indians seemed to travel a great deal, and were always getting on and off trains. They were an unusually handsome tribe, and the women wore very pretty costumes.

Finally a day came when our driver, a Carlisle College Indian named Mr. Sarascino, announced that he could get us to Ácoma. There is no need to tell of that journey—Willa Cather has told it in the *Archbishop*. In a sense, she had been looking forward to it all her life. As we passed the Mesa Encantada (the Enchanted Bluff) we stopped for a long time to look up at it. A great cloud-mesa hung over it. It looked lonely and mysterious and remote, as if it were far distant in time—thousands of years away.

Death Comes for the Archbishop was published in the Fall of 1927. It was so unlike anything else Willa Cather had written, and so unlike anything at all that was being written, the publishers were not prepared for its instant and overwhelming success; and for a time it ran out of stock, and booksellers could not supply the demand for it.

Among the hundreds of letters she got about it, there were a great many interesting ones from nuns and priests; some of the older priests who wrote to her had known Archbishop Lamy and Bishop Machebeuf, the prototypes of *Archbishop Latour* and *Father Vaillant*. The reception of the book by Catholics was very gratifying to Willa Cather. It would have deeply hurt her pride if her representation of Catholic thought and feeling had been considered by them inaccurate or superficial or misleading. Not being herself a Catholic, it had been an enterprise of considerable boldness to write a narrative of French Catholic priests from their own point of view. But all her life she had been profoundly interested in Catholicism— especially in the Catholicism of the Middle Ages, of the time of Abelard and St. Bernard. She had read widely on the subject long before she came to write the *Archbishop*. And she had known well many Catholic priests. Father Fitzgerald, the resident priest in Red Cloud, had been her friend from childhood.

One of her friends of early Pittsburgh days was Ewan Macpherson, a Scotsman born in Jamaica, who had been educated for the priesthood at Stonyhurst. He never became a priest, but he was a fine scholar, with a thorough knowledge of Catholic tradition. After editing a small magazine in Pittsburgh (Willa

Cather and George Seibel were its chief contributors) he came to New York and took a position with the Catholic Encyclopedia. I recall the long talks Willa Cather used to have with him, about Newman, and about St. Augustine. As she intimates in her letter to *The Commonweal*, she did not "soak herself in Catholic lore" in order to write *Death Comes for the Archbishop;* but she drew on a large accumulated store of thought and knowledge.

The publication of the *Archbishop* marked, in a way, the close of an era in Willa Cather's life; for that Fall we were obliged to leave 5 Bank Street—the building was to be torn down. I think Willa Cather did her happiest writing in the fifteen years she lived there. It was there that she completed *O Pioneers!*, and worked at all her other books through *Death Comes for the Archbishop*. Although she wrote parts of them in other places—chiefly Jaffrey and Grand Manan—they all came back to 5 Bank Street, it was there they had their home. Those years from 1912 to 1927 were for her years of absorbing and delightful experiment and discovery. All the time she was steadily developing her powers as an artist, and I think the consciousness of this gave her the deepest contentment and satisfaction.

The financial rewards that came to her were of course gratifying, in that they freed her from worry about money and assured her of liberty to work with complete independence. She liked, too, being able to make generous gifts to a great many people:—old women out on Nebraska farms, her family, her friends. But in other ways money was less important to her than to the majority of people. She had genuinely simple tastes. I think luxury was actually distasteful to her. She never wished much for personal possessions. There was one exception—she was greatly attracted by beautiful jewels; but she never bought any. I think they would have been spoiled for her by the thought of what the money would mean to some of her old friends in the West.

During the time that Willa Cather was living at 5 Bank Street there were none of those breaks in her family circle which later saddened her life. All her brothers and sisters were alive, and her father and mother lived happily and contentedly in their house in Red Cloud, seeing a great deal of their grandchildren and their neighbours. Margie, the old family servant from Virginia, was still with them—at least, for the greater part of this period. Nothing changed very much. When she went home for visits—and she went again and again, stopping off on her journeys back from the Southwest, spending Christmas in Red Cloud, sometimes spending the entire summer there—

she found many of the old friends she had always known; older, but living very much the same lives. Above all, she found her own home and her father and mother the same. It was like finding her childhood and early youth again. When she wrote those often-quoted passages in the last part of the *Archbishop*—of how, in New Mexico, he always awoke a young man—I think she was transferring to him something of her own feeling about waking in the morning in Red Cloud.

In the next four years, both her father and mother died, and that part of her life vanished forever.

12 *"Shadows on the Rock"*

IT was her discovery of France on this continent that led to Willa Cather's novel *Shadows on the Rock*.

She had long been a reader of Francis Parkman. She found him the most interesting of American historians. But his chronicles of the French in Quebec had never, I think, given her any particular impulse to visit that province. Perhaps she thought of modern Quebec as too far separated in time and place from the France she loved to have much left of its original character. Our going there in the summer of 1928 came about by chance.

On leaving 5 Bank Street, Willa Cather had taken refuge in the Grosvenor Hotel, at 10th Street and 5th Avenue, a few steps from Washington Square, and across the street from the Church of the Ascension, her favourite church in New York; she loved the beautiful altar, with John La Farge's great fresco above; and for years went regularly to the vesper services, where the organist, Miss Jessie Craig Adam, a Scots-woman, conducted one of the best-trained small choirs in New York. Percy Grant, that picturesque figure, was the rector then. I recall how once, before he ever met Willa Cather, he sent a messenger to 5 Bank Street, with an urgent invitation for her to *breakfast* with him!

When Willa Cather moved to the Grosvenor, she regarded it as a merely temporary expedient. The small, sunless rooms at the back of the hotel had the advantage of quiet; but otherwise they were simply a place to sleep and keep one's trunks. But family affairs for a long time necessitated her travelling back and forth across the continent; it seemed impracticable to make any more permanent living arrangements, and for nearly five years the Grosvenor was Willa Cather's only New York residence.

That Fall she went out to Nebraska to spend Christmas with her father and mother. While she was there her father had a first attack of angina. In March, soon after her return to New York, she got the news of his sudden death.

It was a great shock to her—not only the personal loss, but her realization of the changes it foreshadowed. There had always been the kindest and fondest relationship between her and her father; and his gentle, modest pride in her achievements, and the high esteem they had won, were one of the chief satisfactions she got from what is known as success.

She took the train again to Red Cloud for his funeral. There was a large, exhausting family gathering; and her brother Douglass persuaded his mother, worn out with the strain, to go back with him to California for a long rest.

I remember how, that summer, Grand Manan seemed the only foothold left on earth. With all her things in storage—with not even a comfortable writing-table to write at—Willa Cather looked forward fervently to her attic at Grand Manan. No palace could have seemed so attractive to her just then as that rough little cottage, with the soft fogs blowing across the flowery fields, and the crystalline quiet of the place. We decided to go this time by the roundabout way of Quebec, in order to try a new route and see some new country.

But from the first moment that she looked down from the windows of the Frontenac on the pointed roofs and Norman outlines of the town of Quebec, Willa Cather was not merely stirred and charmed— she was overwhelmed by the flood of memory, recognition, surmise it called up; by the sense of its extraordinarily French character, isolated and kept intact through hundreds of years, as if by a miracle, on this great un-French continent.

Perhaps by a fortunate accident, I came down with a sudden attack of influenza the night we arrived, and had to stay in bed; and Willa Cather went roaming alone about the town during most of the ten days we spent there. She visited the Ursuline Convent, the Cathedral, the great Laval Seminary, the Church of Our Lady of Victory, the market-place in the Lower Town; and brought back, I remember, thrilling accounts of them all. After I recovered, we made an excursion together to the Île d'Orléans. The Frontenac, where we were stopping, had an excellent library of Canadian history, including the works of Parkman. Willa Cather now re-read his Canadian histories, and some of the other volumes she found there. One of these was a book by the Abbé Scott, who had a parish not far from Quebec. It interested her so much that through M. Giroux, a Canadian book collector with whom she made friends, and who was afterwards of valuable assistance to her in helping her look up historical sources, she arranged to go and call on the Abbé Scott. She found him a most cultivated and distinguished scholar, living secluded off there in the Canadian wilds. She told with enthusiasm of his beautiful Latin library, bound in vellum, and the charm of his little house, where he sometimes entertained visiting priests.

I have sometimes thought that Willa Cather's great pleasure in this Quebec visit came from finding here a sort of continuation, in a different key, of the Catholic theme which had absorbed her for two years, and which still lingered in her thoughts, after the completion of the *Archbishop*, like a tune that goes on in one's mind after the song is ended. Dickens, in his preface to *David Copperfield*, tells "how sorrowfully the pen is laid down at the close of a two years' imaginative task." I think Willa Cather never got so much happiness from the writing of any book as from the *Archbishop*; and although *Shadows on the Rock* is of course altogether different in conception, in treatment, and in artistic purpose, it may have been in part a reluctance to leave that world of Catholic feeling and tradition in which she had lived so happily for so long that led her to embark on this new novel.

That summer at Grand Manan, I do not remember her talking much about Quebec. She rarely discussed in advance anything she intended to write. Occasionally she outlined beforehand her plan for a novel; but she always left out its real theme, the secret treasure at its heart, the thing that gave it its reason for being. She sometimes spoke of her father that summer. I

think her mind often went back to his gentle protectiveness and kindness, the trusting relationship between them, in the old days in Virginia. Something of
that perhaps entered into her conception of the
apothecary *Euclide Auclair* and his little daughter.

So far as I recollect, Willa Cather began writing
Shadows on the Rock that Fall at the Grosvenor. At
Thanksgiving she made a second visit to Quebec, this
time alone. She was working with the energy and concentration she always brought to a new undertaking
when, in December, she got word that her mother in
California had had a paralytic stroke; and broke off
her writing to hurry to the Coast and help her brother
Douglass make arrangements for their mother's care.

The long illness of Mrs. Cather—it lasted two and
a half years—had a profound effect on Willa Cather,
and I think on her work as well. She had come to
understand her mother better and better through the
years—her strong-willed, imperious nature, full of
quick, eager impulses—quick to resent, quick to
sympathize, headstrong, passionate, and yet capable of
great kindness and understanding. She realized with
complete imagination what it meant for a proud
woman like her mother to lie month after month
quite helpless, unable to speak articulately, although
her mind was perfectly clear. In Willa Cather's long

stays in Pasadena, where her mother was cared for in a sanatorium, she had to watch her continually growing weaker, more ailing, yet unable to die. It was one of those experiences that make a lasting change in the climate of one's mind.

Mrs. Cather was lodged in a little cottage of the sanatorium, with a nurse, and was visited daily all through her illness by her son Douglass, who had always been devoted to her; and from time to time by her other children, who came on from Nebraska and Wyoming. For a year or more her interest in life, even her quick sense of humour, was still keen; she enjoyed hearing all the family news, especially the slightest incidents relating to her grandchildren. At Pasadena Willa Cather was able to rent a separate cottage in the sanatorium grounds, and to do some writing. She could not work there on *Shadows on the Rock;* but she wrote most of the short story *Two Friends,* and I think began *Old Mrs. Harris* there.

Carrying on a sustained piece of imaginative work under these conditions was of course difficult; but at the same time Willa Cather found in it a great release. To write about the period she had chosen, she had to do a considerable amount of reading and historical research; and this she could quite well do in the small apartment at the Grosvenor, which did not offer many other resources. I recall with what pleasure and absorption she read the Jesuit *Relations,* and Lahontan's *Voyages,* and re-read the *Memoirs* of Saint-Simon. One day she went out and bought some full-size copies of the *Lady and Unicorn* tapestries which hang in the Cluny Museum, and had them hung at the foot of her bed, so that when she was reading in bed at night she could look up at them instead of at the blank hotel walls.

On New Year's Eve we made another trip to Quebec, through country deep in snow. Early in 1930 Willa Cather travelled West again to visit her mother. In May we sailed for France.

I remember our stay there as a happy one, in spite of the anxieties that shadowed it: the illness of Mrs. Cather, and the beginning of Isabelle Hambourg's long illness. For two months Willa Cather followed the trail of Count Frontenac in Paris. She used to walk often along the Quai des Célestins and about Frontenac's old quarter; she visited the church of St. Paul, and Saint-Nicholas-des-Champs, where Frontenac's heart was buried; and spent many mornings at the Musée Carnavalet, looking up things she wanted to know. With Jan and Isabelle Hambourg she made a short trip to St. Malo. There had been a tremendous storm the night before, the greatest for twenty years along that coast, and the sea was flinging great waves over the sea-wall. Weather was always a very positive element in Willa Cather's consciousness. She had a poet's attitude toward weather, to her it was one of the rich, contributive constituents of life. It is interesting to note how much weather plays a part in the Quebec story.

From Paris we travelled south, with rather a sense of leaving all care behind; drifting slowly down through the Provençal country. It was the part of France Willa Cather loved best, she was always lighterhearted in the south. We ended up at Aix-les-Bains, where the wonderful adventure with Madame Grout, Flaubert's niece Caroline, took place.

The little hotel at Aix-les-Bains where Willa Cather had stayed before had disappeared; so we went first to the Splendide, and were given an extremely large and beautiful and luxurious room, with three balconies, and a superb view overlooking the lake. But Willa Cather had a great distaste for luxury hotels; she did not want to stop along with King Alfonso and the Agha Khan (who were both registered there), or to dine on a terrace with lighted orange-trees to the music of an orchestra. She was extremely gloomy and discontented, even resentful, the first day or two, as if she had been cheated out of all the things she had come back to Aix-les-Bains to find. It was not until we removed to the plain, old-fashioned Grand Hotel down in the town, which she learned about through the English bank, that she recovered her happy spirits. If we had not gone there, we should never, of course, have had the encounter with Mme. Grout, which Willa Cather tells so memorably in *A Chance Meeting*.

It was not, I believe, from any plan relating to her work, but as a matter of practical convenience that Willa Cather decided to return to America by one of the Empress boats, which docked at Quebec. But the whole voyage became a sort of home-coming to *Shadows*, and the slow progress up the St. Lawrence, between woods on fire with October, was its climax— a dream of joy. It had been Willa Cather's intention to go straight on to Boston and Jaffrey; but although her luggage had gone on ahead, she instantly decided to buy warm clothes and stay at the Frontenac for a while. (During this stay she for the first time visited the Hôpital Général, and saw Bishop de Saint-Vallier's two small, poor rooms where he humbly ended his life.) Everything she experienced brought her closer and closer to her story, and when she did finally start for Jaffrey, she could hardly wait to be at her writing-table again. She wrote the last part of *Shadows* very rapidly, part of it at Jaffrey, part at the Grosvenor, finishing it December 27th.

One curious accident, which almost became a catastrophe, happened in connection with the text of *Shadows.* Willa Cather was always very painstaking about her facts—she intensely disliked being careless or inaccurate, and went to much trouble to verify them. Occasionally, of course, she made slips. In the short story, *Two Friends,* she spoke of the "transit of Venus," and several astronomers wrote her that it could not have been a transit of Venus at that date, and must have been an "occlusion of Venus." (She was writing of a childhood experience, and her Red Cloud neighbours had called it a transit of Venus; it did not occur to her to look it up.) In the *Archbishop* she described the water at Arroyo Hondo as running up-hill in open wooden troughs, and was reproached for it sadly by one or two engineers. This was an error of observation, and she corrected it in later editions.

She read carefully the copy of *Shadows* and then the galley and page proofs. In early March she left for California, to visit her mother, and to receive a degree from the University of California, asking me, before she went, to look over the foundry proofs when they came in. I believe it is not customary to send the author foundry proofs—any changes, of course, after the type is locked in the forms, are very expensive. But she always asked to see them.

While I was reading them, I got a telegram from her, saying that throughout the story *Archbishop* Laval and *Archbishop* de Saint-Vallier must be changed to *Bishop* Laval and *Bishop* de Saint-Vallier. It must have been through pure absent-mindedness that she made this mistake, for she knew the correct titles and had seen them hundreds of times in print—and so had I! But she had got used to writing the word Archbishop. In San Francisco, while she was there for her degree, she happened to show an old friend, a Catholic, some of the proofs she had with her; and this friend instantly noticed the error, fortunately being well up in Catholic history. If it had gone through, it would have been endlessly annoying and humiliating; probably half the Catholics who read the book would have written to correct it.

Willa Cather received two honorary degrees that year; the degree of Doctor of Laws from the University of California in March, and of Doctor of Letters from Princeton in June. She greatly enjoyed meeting Nicholas Murray Butler again at the California commencement; he shepherded her through it with a sort of special protectiveness and admiration. And at Princeton, where she was treated by everyone with the highest honour and consideration (she was the first woman to be given a degree by Princeton) she was deeply interested in meeting and talking with Charles Lindbergh and his wife. The clerk at her drugstore had once said to her: "He's the boy of the U.S.A. for me!" She always liked that saying.

But in spite of her genuine pleasure in these two commencements, and in spite of the great success of *Shadows on the Rock,* the year 1931 was a very hard one— it took something permanently from her vital force. She was about three months in California, with her mother steadily failing. In the summer, at Grand Manan, she got the word of her mother's death. It meant the final breaking up of the family and the Red Cloud home, for it was the father and mother who had held it together all these years, it was to them the children and grandchildren all came back. After their going, the family as a family might almost be said not to exist any longer, but only personal relationships between the different members.

That Christmas Willa Cather did make a final visit to Red Cloud, a sort of leave-taking of all her past there. She opened the old house, and got back a former favourite housekeeper to stay with her. She saw her old friends and neighbours, and had some of her family come to visit her. And she made a journey, over snow-blocked roads, to see My Ántonia again— one of her happiest remembrances.

She had become very tired of living in a hotel, with her clothes in trunks, all her pictures and books in storage, no real place to see or entertain her friends. The loss of her father and mother, the loss of Red Cloud, the loss of 5 Bank Street, the long exhausting journeys back and forth across the continent, a general sense of homelessness and uprootedness, had affected her health and her spirits. Yet I think there is no indication of this in her essay, *A Chance Meeting*, which she wrote in the spring at the Grosvenor.

Perhaps it is not until one can get a long perspective that life falls into a composition, like that of a story or a musical creation; at the time one is too much engaged in living it to take much account of its form or direction. Looking back, it seems to me that for Willa Cather the fifteen years at Bank Street were a continuous ascent in artistic accomplishment, a period of high vitality and great momentum, culminating in her finest work, *Death Comes for the Archbishop*. During the five years at the Grosvenor, I believe that momentum was checked—never again to regain its former drive. Whether without the saddening changes, the physical and spiritual strain of those years, the arrow would have gone higher and higher, it is useless to speculate. Every arrow must sometime begin to fall. It was Willa Cather's nature to put life before any theory of life. She lived by vital impulse, not by intellectual choices. She did not choose between her work and her feeling for the needs, the claims of her family and friends. Her work was herself, and whatever the issue she had to meet, she met it with her whole self—never held back part for other uses. If her writing had to suffer, it had to suffer.

Stephen Tennant, in his distinguished Preface to *Willa Cather on Writing*, has said: "She loved faithfulness. . . . She gave the impression of one who has gazed deep and long into the crystal of human fidelity." Perhaps in that crystal she found the mirror of her own strongest instinct. She had not one of those divided natures that sometimes turn on themselves and what they have cherished, that hate where they love, and find in betrayal itself an ultimate truth; though she could comprehend and portray such a nature in Myra Henshaw, in *My Mortal Enemy*. All her impulses were simple, direct, unswerving, as if they came from some changeless center of integrity.

Again and again, in the years that followed, it was not so much that she put her work aside, as that the current of life swept her away from it, to answer some, to her, compelling call of friendship, of affection, of compassion, of responsibility. It was temperamentally impossible for her to remain inactive, contemplative, where the misfortunes of her friends were concerned.

I remember one incident long ago when we were living at 5 Bank Street. A faithful scrub-woman who used to come to us lost her husband, and became very hysterical and unbalanced about it. Her relatives promptly put her into an institution for the insane. Willa Cather, when she heard of it, at once dropped the work she was doing, wrote forcible letters to the heads of the institution, telephoned influential friends, and got her out; after which Mrs. Winn, as she was called, went on being a faithful scrub-woman. It was not benevolence or a sense of duty, it was a flash of purely personal feeling that moved Willa Cather then, as always, in all such acts; the complete, imaginative understanding of another's dilemma, and the instant need to succor it, to give all her powers, if need be, to dealing with it.

The long tragic illness of Isabelle McClung, the death of her favourite brothers, Douglass and Roscoe (whom she had confidently expected to outlive her, since they were both younger than she), the time and strength and expense of spirit she put into following and assisting their fortunes, undoubtedly, I think, lessened Willa Cather's literary production in the later years. In some artists, perhaps, life and work are two dual streams, one flows on more or less independently of the other. Scott, I believe, wrote some of his finest novels in a time of greatest suffering and adversity. But Scott was an impersonal writer; and he had a giant vitality.

It seems to me that it is in this quality of vitality that Willa Cather's last three novels—*Shadows on the Rock, Lucy Gayheart, Sapphira and the Slave Girl*—differ from those that go before. All her great qualities as an artist remain unchanged. And in the three stories published under the title *Obscure Destinies* one still feels the full flood of her power. But these were shorter works and did not demand the long-sustained effort of a novel.

In the Fall of 1932 we began looking for an apartment, and found one on Park Avenue—the nearest approach we could make to 5 Bank Street. I remember the pleasure Willa Cather got from being reunited with all the rather humble things buried so long in storage vaults, and also in getting a few new furnishings for the new apartment. It was not until December that we moved into it. A couple of weeks later, Josephine, our former French housekeeper, came back to us. It was like beginning really to live again.

13

"Lucy Gayheart" and "Sapphira and the Slave Girl"

ONE of the greatest pleasures that came to Willa Cather in later years was her friendship with the Menuhin family.

She first met the Menuhins in Paris, in the summer of 1930, through Jan Hambourg; Marutha Menuhin and the two little girls, Hephzibah and Yaltah, came to see her at the Grosvenor after she got back, and her intimacy with the family advanced very rapidly. In the spring of 1931, while she was in California, Yehudi was there with his father, giving concerts. It was then that she really came to know Yehudi, and he her; and there began one of those rare, devoted, and unclouded friendships between them that lighted all the years that followed.

She loved the Menuhin family as a whole, and each separate member of it individually. She intensely admired Marutha Menuhin; and she found the two little girls—Yaltah was about seven, and Hephzibah a year or two older—endlessly captivating, amusing, and endearing. She had always had a delight in children; when she was growing up in Red Cloud, she had been passionately fond of her youngest brother and sister, Jack and Elsie. Afterwards she had something of the same attachment for her young nieces and her nephew Charles Cather. When her brother Roscoe's twin daughters were babies, and she went out to Wyoming to visit him, she never tired of playing with them. She played with children, not as if she were a grown person, but as children play—with the same spirit of experiment, of adventurousness and unreflecting enjoyment.

The three Menuhin children had had a very strict bringing up. Surrounded on all sides by the curiosity and adulation and publicity which try to break into and take possession of any popular form of talent, they lived almost as simply and secludedly as the princes in the Tower must have done. They had lessons and practising the greater part of each day. They took walks with their mother—sometimes as early as half-past six in the morning—in Central Park. They almost never went to other peoples' houses; but they were allowed to be present at the frequent gatherings of friends in the Menuhins' own hotel apartments. The little girls were always dressed very plainly until they began to grow up—perhaps because of this, they had an extravagant admiration for pretty clothes. In their mother's box at the concerts they usually appeared in little navy blue serge dresses, with navy blue caps on their golden heads. I remember how rapturously they told, once, of some inexpensive trinkets their mother had bought for them in Germany; and how Hephzibah, who was then about nine, declared with fervour: "To me, a woman without jewels is not a woman."

They were not only the most gifted children Willa Cather had ever known, with that wonderful aura of imaginative charm, prescience, inspiration, that even the most gifted lose after they grow up; they were also extremely lovable, affectionate, and unspoiled; in some ways funnily naive, in others sensitive and discerning far beyond their years. They had an immense capacity for admiration and hero-worship, and Willa Cather became, I think, their greatest hero.

I remember the Menuhin family's winter visits to New York, in the years that followed, as a sort of continuous festival, full of concerts and gay parties; orange trees and great baskets of flowers for Willa Cather arriving in the midst of snow-storms; birthday luncheons, with Russian caviare and champagne; excursions to the opera, where she took Yaltah and Hephzibah to hear *Parsifal* for the first time; long walks around the reservoir in Central Park, when the three children all wanted to walk beside her, and had to take turnabout. They discussed very abstract subjects together—art, religion, philosophy, life. If Willa Cather had been writing *War and Peace,* I am sure she would have abandoned it to take these walks.

She had a feeling that Hephzibah and Yaltah, travelling in so many countries, and learning something of the language of each, were never going to get a thorough sense of the English language; and this worried her. She asked Marutha Menuhin if she might organize a Shakespeare Club, with no one allowed to be present except herself and the little girls. Yehudi then asked if he might come too. They began with *Richard II,* and went on to *Macbeth* and *Henry IV.* Willa Cather hunted through the bookstores of New York to get each of the children a copy of these plays in the original Temple Edition, the only one she herself cared to read; it was then rapidly going out of print.

She was greatly touched when, many years afterward, Yehudi told her he had found and bought a complete second-hand set of the Temple Shakespeare, in a shop in New Orleans.

The last in all that long procession of joyous meetings took place a month or two before Willa Cather's death, when Hephzibah, on a visit to this country

from Australia, telephoned one morning to ask if
she might bring her husband and her two little boys
to the Park Avenue apartment and introduce them.
(A night or two before, Hephzibah and Yehudi had
played a concert at the Metropolitan, and Willa
Cather, though it was an effort that winter for her
to go out in the evening, had managed to hear them.)
Not long after Hephzibah and her family arrived,
Yehudi turned up, with his little son and daughter.
Once again the apartment was filled with children's
voices and laughter. Under all the gaiety and happiness of that morning, there was somehow a sense of
heartbreak. Hephzibah wrote afterwards that she felt
from the first she would never see their beloved Aunt
Willa again. When it drew toward noon, Yehudi said
gently that they must be going, since he and Hephzibah were sailing for England at one o'clock, and he
had to take his children home first. It was the first
word that had been spoken of their sailing.

After she moved into the Park Avenue apartment,
music, and all the associations that went with it, became Willa Cather's greatest recreation and enjoyment. The old heroic days of opera seemed to have
gone forever; but she heard a great many concerts,
both symphony concerts and concerts of chamber
music. Soon after she was settled, Blanche and Alfred

Knopf presented her with an extremely fine phonograph. It gave her endless pleasure. Yehudi sent her from England all the records he had made with Hephzibah; and she bought records of the last Beethoven quartets, and dozens of others of her favourite compositions. She loved playing these records to Ethel Litchfield, her dear friend of Pittsburgh days, who had now come to New York to live, and who dined with us nearly every week. Through Ethel Litchfield she met Josef Lhevinne; she hardly ever missed one of his concerts. She also greatly enjoyed seeing Myra Hess when she came over from England on concert tours. They had met first at the Alfred Knopfs, and had become warm friends.

Perhaps it was in part the happiness of living again in an atmosphere of music—she heard scarcely any music during the Grosvenor period—that gave Willa Cather the theme of *Lucy Gayheart*. She began working at it in the spring of 1933. She did not attack it with any great vigour or enthusiasm; she had not recovered from the strain of the preceding years, and often wrote "very tired," "deadly tired" in the 'Line-a-day' she commenced about this time. But I think she felt that whatever its faults, the story had reality, that it was rooted deep in her experience, and that she wanted to tell it. (Several years before, she had talked of writing a story about a girl like Lucy; she was going to call it *Blue Eyes on the Platte*.)

She worked at intervals that summer at Grand Manan; but it was not until she went to Jaffrey in the Fall that she began to feel again a sense of physical well-being and plenitude. Her letters, written soon after she got there, were full of the pleasure of sleeping deeply in that cool mountain air, of waking with the thought of the quiet woods beneath her; of feeling hungry all the time; and of being able to live with her story. She wrote the latter part of *Lucy Gayheart* as fast as her pencil could move across the paper. When she considered sending the manuscript to New York to be typed, she finally decided not to, because she was "too afraid of loss in the most registered of mails." She could never write it again, she declared; the conditions would never again be so good.

In the months that followed, she began to type her hand-written copy, making changes and revisions as she went along. But now there befell the greatest working calamity of her career. Her right wrist began to be painfully swollen; and when she went one day to the doctor with it, he diagnosed it as a serious inflammation of the sheath of the tendon, and said the hand must be completely immobilized. From this time on she was never free from the threat of this disability, which attacked sometimes her right hand, and less frequently her left. Often for months to-gether she had to wear the steel and leather brace that Dr. Frank Ober, the great orthopedic surgeon, devised for her; it immobilized her thumb, but left her fingers free, so that she was able with some diffi-culty to sign her name, or to trace a few words at the end of a dictated letter. All this meant that for long periods she was unable to do any writing—she could not even typewrite. She never tried to dictate a piece of creative work. She felt it to be, for her, a psycho-logical impossibility.

Although this affliction made the simplest acts of life, which ordinarily one performs unconsciously—taking a bath, dressing oneself, tying a knot, opening a letter—wearisomely difficult and irksome, Willa Cather rarely let it depress her spirits or affect her independence. I remember her telling once, when someone offered to help her, how when she was a very little child, and her parents would try to assist her in something, she would protest passionately: "Self-alone, self-alone!"

In the spring of 1934, her hand had sufficiently re-covered for her to begin to work again, and she fin-ished the typing and copy-reading of *Lucy Gayheart*, and read the proofs at Grand Manan. (She kept an old Oliver typewriter at Grand Manan, which the garage-man, the only mechanic on the Island, used to repair for her when it broke down. I was amused, not long ago, reading an article on Paul Valéry by his son, to find that Valéry too used an old Oliver type-writer to type his manuscripts.) In Jaffrey, that Fall, she began a new piece of work—not a novel, but a "long short story," which she planned to be about the same length as *Old Mrs. Harris*. Its title was *The Golden Wedding*. With the exception of the Avignon story, on which she was working at the time of her death, it was, so far as I can recall, the only thing she ever began that she did not finish.

Life had somehow broken up the continuity of effort that characterized the Bank Street years. In those years Willa Cather had accepted physical discomforts, all the makeshifts and deprivations a severe economy imposes, with great buoyancy, even with zest. It was very difficult to heat the Bank Street apartment. One very cold winter, when there was a general shortage of coal, I remember her hiring the grocer's boy across the street to go down with her to the docks and bring back his hand-cart full of coal, since none of the coal dealers would take any orders. She happened to mention to D. H. Lawrence that she always kept her flowers in the bath-room at night. "Bath-room the coldest room in the house?" he asked quickly. She rarely felt that she could afford a cab, and would walk long distances in the bitter wind to get a bus. When we went to the opera in the evening, we generally rode on the Seventh Avenue streetcar; often our fellow-passengers were the jolly Italian wine-dealer and his wife from whom we bought supplies. They were old friends of Caruso, and he always sent them tickets for his performances.

No hardships, no interruptions or annoyances, no worries even, impeded the strong, sure flow of her central interest and determination in those years. It bore them along as sticks and leaves are borne on the current of a stream.

After she moved into the apartment on Park Avenue, she enjoyed a comfort and quiet, a protection from outside intrusion, she had never known before; freedom from any care about money; ease and prestige and consideration, and great pleasure in friendship. But she did not get back that power to work which comes from the sense of limitless reserves of strength, to use or throw away.

I think her friendships came to mean more and more to her in the years that followed. One of the friendships that counted most for her was that with her English friend Stephen Tennant, youngest son of Lord and Lady Glenconner. He had written to her

about *A Lost Lady* while he was still a student at the
Slade School in London. They had corresponded
ever since. She kept all his letters—the only ones she
kept like this, except Miss Jewett's. His visits to
America about this time gave her a kind of stimulus
and delight entirely new; for he was the only one
among the new generation of writers with whom she
could talk about writing on an absolutely equal
plane, with complete freedom and—though their
views were in many ways so different—with complete
sympathy and accord. On one of his visits he told
her how warmly Thomas Hardy had spoken to him
of *A Lost Lady*. I think no other tribute ever gave her
so much pleasure, for she admired Hardy as the greatest of living novelists.

Willa Cather did no writing at all in 1935; the
greater part of the year was taken up with services for
Isabelle Hambourg, who came, desperately ill, to
America that spring, with her husband, the violinist.
Willa Cather got rooms for them in a near-by hotel,
had her own doctor examine Mrs. Hambourg (he
pronounced her illness incurable, and said she must
go at once to a hospital), made all the hospital arrangements, visited her every day; and when, later, her
condition improved, and she insisted on accompanying
her husband to Chicago, on a musical project he had

in mind, Willa Cather went with them, to lighten the journey as much as possible. From late March until August, when they sailed, all her time was given to the Hambourgs. She spent six weeks in Venice that summer. Afterwards she rejoined the Hambourgs in Paris, to give them what help and pleasure she could. She was there for two months. It was the last time she saw Isabelle Hambourg, who died three years later in Sorrento.

In 1925 Willa Cather had offered to make a collection of Miss Jewett's best stories, and write a preface for a new edition if Houghton Mifflin would publish it. She now suggested to Alfred Knopf that she collect the critical essays she had written, including this Preface, and publish them in a volume. *The Novel Démeublé* had appeared some years before in the *New Republic*, her article on Mrs. Fields in the Boston *Transcript*, *A Chance Meeting* in the *Atlantic Monthly*, the Katherine Mansfield article in the Borzoi 1925. Knopf very much wished her to write something on Thomas Mann's *Joseph and His Brothers*, to be included in the volume; and to please him, she did so. She spent part of the spring and summer of 1936 preparing and proof-reading this material, and it was published under the provocative title *Not Under Forty*—which, with her brief explanatory note, got more publicity, I think, than anything else in the book. Several editorials were written about it.

It was no doubt that Fall that she wrote *The Old Beauty,* for she notes copyreading it in February, 1937. At the request of Gertrude Lane, editor of the *Woman's Home Companion,* who had published *Lucy Gayheart* serially, as well as several of Willa Cather's short stories, Willa Cather sent her *The Old Beauty.* She did not much like serial publication, but she liked Miss Lane, liked her honesty and downrightness. Miss Lane said at once that she would publish the story, but that she could not feel the enthusiasm for it she felt for Miss Cather's other work. So Willa Cather asked her to return it. She put it aside for inclusion in a book of short stories, if she should publish one later. She herself thought highly of *The Old Beauty.* She had found it interesting to write, and she felt that she had carried through her idea successfully.

As early as 1932, Maxwell Perkins, of *Charles Scribner's Sons,* had written to Alfred Knopf, proposing the publication by *Scribner's* of a complete limited edition of Willa Cather's work, to be sold through their subscription department. (Knopf did not publish subscription editions.)"Certainly," Mr. Perkins wrote,"if there is any distinction in this form of publication, she of all Americans is entitled to it." The offer he made was a very liberal one.

Houghton Mifflin, however, who held the rights on Willa Cather's first four books, felt that the subscription edition should be theirs; they too then made her an offer, and after considerable negotiation, Willa Cather gave her consent, and Houghton Mifflin began publishing the definitive edition in 1937. They engaged Bruce Rogers to design the format, and took the greatest pains with every detail; and Willa Cather also gave a great deal of time and conscientious effort to it, though it was not the kind of work she really liked; she would far rather have been writing a new story. She made a number of corrections, but I think few radical changes in the text, except in the case of *The Song of the Lark;* there she cut very freely; she had always, in later years, disliked some of the more flowery passages. She also cut the introduction to *My Ántonia* by more than half.

It was three years since she had been engaged on a novel. She greatly missed the companionship of a long piece of work, the feeling of unity and purpose and inner richness it gave to life. That Fall she began *Sapphira and the Slave Girl.*

She had often been urged to write a Virginia novel; but for a long time some sort of inhibition—a reluctance, perhaps, to break through to those old memories that seemed to belong to another life—had deterred her; though she sometimes spoke of incidents, stories of the Virginia years, which she might write about some day.

I think it was the death of her father and mother, and the long train of associations and memories their death set in motion that led her to write *Sapphira*. Virginia, which she had not given much thought to during all the Bank Street period, had come to occupy her mind more and more. When she did finally begin the writing of *Sapphira*, it was with her whole power and concentration.

In the spring of 1938 she proposed going down to Winchester for a couple of weeks and visiting again the old places.

It was as memorable an experience, as intense and thrilling in its way, as those journeys in New Mexico, when she was writing the *Archbishop*. Every bud and leaf and flower seemed to speak to her with a peculiar poignancy, every slope of the land, every fence and wall, rock and stream. I remember how she spoke of the limp, drooping acacia trees in bloom along all the roadsides—how they had the shiftless look that characterized so many Southern things, but how their wood was the toughest of all, and was in great demand for fence-posts. She found again the wild azalea growing on the gravelly banks of the road up Timber Ridge, and gathered great bunches of it. The dogwood, in the almost leafless woods, had a dazzling beauty that spring. Her delight in these things gave, I think, a great freshness of detail to *Sapphira*.

The countryside was very much changed. But she refused to look at its appearance; she looked through and through it, as if it were transparent, to what she knew as its reality. Willowshade, her old home, had been bought by a man* who had always borne a sort of grudge against the place; he chopped down the great willow trees that gave Willowshade its name, and destroyed the high box hedges that seemed so wonderful to Willa Cather when she was a child. The house itself had become so ruinous and forlorn that she did not go into it, only stood and looked down at it from a distance. All these transformations, instead of disheartening her, seemed to light a fierce inner flame that illumined all her pictures of the past.

In writing the story, it was the flooding force of a great wealth of impressions that she had to control. She could have written two or three *Sapphiras* out of her material; and in fact she did write, in her first draft, twice as much as she used. She always said it was what she left out that counted.

*It now belongs to a new owner.

It was a novel written against circumstance. One catastrophe after another blocked its path; the sudden death of her brother Douglass—the most bitter, I think, of all her losses; the death of Isabelle Hambourg; the second World War. Many people thought she was "not interested" in the war; but, indeed, she felt it too much to make it the subject of casual conversation. When the French army surrendered, she wrote in her 'Line-a-day', "There seems to be no future at all for people of my generation."

Even Jaffrey, which she had always found such a happy refuge, was largely spoiled for her by the great hurricane of 1938, which wrecked the woods for miles around.

Against all these things, she worked at *Sapphira* with a resoluteness, a sort of fixed determination which I think was different from her ordinary working mood; as if she were bringing all her powers into play to save this, whatever else was lost. She often worked far beyond her strength. In the summers of 1938 and 1939 we stayed in New York through the heat until the end of July, because she did not want to interrupt what she was then doing. She finished the story at Grand Manan in September, 1940.

Once in a while, I think, a writer does a novel that is "uncharacteristic," in the sense that one does not find in it the qualities one most looks to find; the qualities that most predominate in the writer's other work. But this, perhaps, sometimes comes not so much from a lack, as from an emergence, a substitution of other latent traits in the writer's development. I believe that *Sapphira* has very strongly the quality of permanence, of survival; and that as time goes on, it will take a higher and higher place in any estimate of Willa Cather's work. It is written austerely, with very little of that warmth and generous expansion of feeling so many of her readers delight in. It is a novel without a heroine—the central figure is a cold and rather repellent character. Nothing is stressed—incidents, scenes are touched on so lightly, one is hardly aware of their having more than a surface significance. Yet one finds—I find, at least—that they have a curiously imperishable quality. The story as a whole seems to me to be the brief chronicle of a time that will never again be recaptured with the same truth and crystalline vision, the same supreme art.

14 *The Last Years*

THE last years were not years of decline, except in a physical sense; they were years, I think, of deeper vision, of a more penetrating sense of human life and human destiny. Willa Cather read and thought a great deal during those years. Her talk never lost its wonderfully incandescent quality, its vividness and fire. She was able to do little writing: for long stretches she could not use her right hand at all; and aside from this great trial, her health became more and more fragile. But those long silences were not vacancies. They were filled with all the harvest of reverie and imagination, the progress of creative thought, out of which works of art are born.

In this later period, when Willa Cather's health more and more limited her activities, one incoming from outside became increasingly a pleasure, and even a sustenance in her life—though it also took something from her. This was her correspondence.

186

The flood of letters which poured in to her from half the countries of the world—letters that were truly from "the people," not from any particular class of people, bringing to her their gratitude, their homage, their affection, in the kind of language she most appreciated—the language art cannot invent—were a sort of giving back to her, a return in kind, of the qualities of feeling she had herself expended in her writing career.

The boy who read her books in Braille, but never referred in his letter to his blindness; the old missionary in New Mexico, who after riding among his parishes all day, sat up until dawn to finish the *Archbishop*; the British officer in Borneo, who wrote: "Your book has been my companion on many a long and weary trip in the jungle, and if I have read it once, I must have read it a hundred times"; the young priest dying in the Italian Dolomites, who wrote: "I beseech you to abide by me in thought and prayer."

"You are a great lady, and we are only poor folk, but I would love to count myself your friend."— "Your books have somehow helped me, a boy from Wisconsin, to take heart again in my effort to rebuild my health and life."—"There is no book, barring the word of God, that has taken so firm a hold on me."— "I hope you have everything fine in this world, Miss

Cather."—"I am glad you are alive, and have written so many splendid books."

She had always been greatly pleased and flattered by the tributes which came to her from distinguished people she admired: the letters, long ago, from President Masaryk, bearing imposing seals, and brought by special messenger from the consulate; Justice Holmes' high praise of *My Ántonia;* what J. M. Barrie and Hardy and many of her literary contemporaries said of her books.

But she had another, and a very strong feeling about these voices that reached her from the unknown, like a great anonymous affirmation of her art.

She tried to answer them all. Her secretary, Miss Sarah Bloom, who for more than twenty years gave her generous, skilful, unfailing service, took care of the routine part of her correspondence. But to these personal letters she dictated replies herself.

In the spring of 1941 she decided to go to California to see her brother Roscoe. Of all her family, Roscoe was the one nearest to her, understood her best. He had felt from the first the promise and importance of her work, and had followed it with faithful sympathy and devotion. They did not often meet, though she visited him several times when he lived in Wyoming. But she had a great wish to keep their lives together;

and her correspondence with this brother told, I think, more about her work and herself than any of her other letters.

Roscoe was seriously ill in the spring of 1941; he had never been strong, and Willa Cather was haunted by the fear that she might never see him again. Although her hand was still in a brace, and she was not well herself, she set out in June, in intense heat, for San Francisco.

She took the Santa Fé from Chicago, and once more made that journey across New Mexico and Arizona she had already travelled so many times—Trinidad, Los Alamos, Lamy, Albuquerque, Gallup, Winslow, the Barstow cutoff. The country had never been more beautiful. The rose acacias were in bloom for miles along the railroad tracks after we left Trinidad. In all the little Mexican villages, one saw the tamarisk, with its long drifts of blossom—the tree Willa Cather had so celebrated in the *Archbishop*. There had been plentiful rains, and everything was fresh and green. She saw it all with tears. She knew it was for the last time.

The San Francisco visit was one of those flawless interludes that seldom happen in life. Roscoe and his wife came in from the country and stayed with Willa Cather at the Fairmont. They spoke of how frail she looked; but she was radiantly happy all through those weeks with her brother.

She had wanted for years to write an Avignon story. On her many journeys to the south of France, it was Avignon that left the deepest impression with her. The Papal Palace at Avignon—seen first when she was a girl—stirred her as no building in the world had ever done. In 1935 we were there together. One day, as we wandered through the great chambers of white, almost translucent stone, alone except for a guide, this young fellow suddenly stopped still in one of the rooms and began to sing, with a beautiful voice. It echoed down the corridors and under the arched ceilings like a great bell sounding—but sounding from some remote past; its vibrations seemed laden, weighted down with the passions of another age— cruelties, splendours, lost and unimaginable to us in our time.

I have sometimes thought that Willa Cather wished to make her story like this song.

She had brought with her to San Francisco Okey's little history of Avignon; and she often spent her mornings on the open roof garden of the Fairmont, walking to and fro, and reading in this book. It was probably then that she planned the general outline of the Avignon story.

From San Francisco she went on to Victoria in British Columbia, which she had always wanted to see. But she seemed less and less strong, and while there scarcely ever left the beautiful gardens of the Empress Hotel where we were stopping. She would sit under a hawthorn tree among the flowering rosebushes, and read; or not even read; the shortest walk tired her.

Canada was already in the war, and the long journey home by the Canadian Pacific, in an old car that had been discarded from service for twenty years, was a trying one. After she got back to New York, she went into the French Hospital for a week to rest.

It is sad to write about illness. Although I recall gay parties in the early months of 1942, music, and happy hours with Yehudi and his wife and children, the greater part of the year was a story of illness. In July, Willa Cather went into the Presbyterian Hospital for a gall-bladder operation. Yehudi came out on the subway to visit her there, and I remember how even her surgeon, the formidable Dr. Whipple (whose chief interest aside from surgery, I believe, was music) unbent and showed a benign pleasure in meeting him.

Although Willa Cather recovered from the operation, she never got back any true health. And yet she never lived the life, or had the manner or appearance of an invalid. Her real self seemed quite untouched by her increasing bodily weakness. To any occasion that moved her strongly, she would rise with full command both of the situation and herself, with all her natural force and ardour.

In the next four years we were unable to go to Grand Manan, because of the war. Ever since the writing of *One of Ours* Willa Cather had found that island, so simple and primitive in all the conditions of living, a great resource, an increasingly congenial place to work. Any complications there were material ones: building a wall to hold up the hillside behind the house; digging an artesian well; dealing with the rats which used to forsake the fish-houses in the Fall and attempt to tunnel under our cottage for warmth; rooting up the black alder, which was always threatening to take the place. The beautiful silence, accentuated instead of diminished by the sound of the sea on the shingle, the wind blowing the alder bushes, rain on the roof, the songs of hundreds of birds, was tranquillizing to the spirit, seemed to open up great spaces for it to roam in.

During the Grosvenor period, Grand Manan was the only spot where Willa Cather could have a few of her own things about her; some of her books, one or two of her rugs which she had sent up from the storage house, a few pieces of silver. She loved homely occupations; took endless pains with the flowers she had planted there; imported a pair of workman's leather gloves, and with her own hands uprooted most of the thistles on the place; performed, with the help of the fisherman who did rough chores for us, a skilful piece of tree surgery, when she found a spruce tree sawing, with one of its branches, into the trunk of a tall birch tree.

It was a sort of Robinson Crusoe life, calling for frequent resourcefulness and invention. One of the principal channels for these qualities—as with Robinson Crusoe—was the quest for food. We often rebelled against the rather austere provision of the only little boardinghouse within reach; so that it was necessary to have a constant stream of supplies winging their way to us from distant points: garlic and olive oil from New York, bread from Montreal, wild strawberry jam from Quebec; and shipments every week from an excellent grocer in St. John, who also sent us, during the Prohibition years in the United States (but Grand Manan was Canadian) Pol Roget of a very good vintage. With these we were able to break the monotony of our fare with splendid banquets, cooked on a little wood-burning range.

But after 1942, Grand Manan no longer seemed possible. Most of the workmen on the Island had gone to the war, or into war industries. The splendid Grand Manan doctor, Dr. Macaulay, a McGill graduate, who had been a staunch friend, and helped us out in any emergency, died of a heart attack. The hardships were too great, unless one had plenty of physical energy. The next four summers Willa Cather spent at Northeast Harbour, Maine.

In these years she made one great literary discovery. The first summer she stayed at Northeast Harbour, it rained a great deal. We were living in a little cottage belonging to the Asticou Inn—a charming place, with a big fireplace in the living room; and since it rained torrents every evening, the best thing to do seemed to be to sit by the fire and read. One evening Willa Cather came over from dinner with her arms piled full of small, thick, brown volumes she had got from the hotel library—a very good one, with all the standard classics. These turned out to be an old Houghton Mifflin edition of Sir Walter Scott.

She had never cared to read Scott. She could remember how, when she was a child, her mother used to ride on horseback to a distant neighbour's to borrow the "Waverley novels" as they slowly found their way across the Atlantic and down into rural Virginia; and in Red Cloud her mother often begged her to read Scott—recalling her own pleasure in his books.

But about this time Willa Cather had just discovered *Anna Karenina;* it seemed to her far more attractive metal than *Old Mortality.* Later, when she was living in Judge McClung's house in Pittsburgh, he too tried to persuade her to become interested in his favourite novelist. He had an unbounded admiration for Scott, enjoying especially his legal passages. It hurt his feelings a little that Willa Cather remained so obdurate. But she had had to teach *Ivanhoe* at school, and thought it one of the dullest and most artificial of books.

Now, however, she began to read, one after another, all the Scottish novels—*Guy Mannering, Rob Roy, The Bride of Lammermoor, Old Mortality, The Heart of Midlothian, The Antiquary, Waverley, Redgauntlet*—and found them a revelation of delight. She talked of them, lived in them. In the succeeding summers we spent at the Asticou Inn, she always re-read them; and in New York she bought herself copies of the ones she liked best. Thinking of her mother and Judge McClung and their entreaties, she planned to write an essay on Scott, which she would call *Apologies in Heaven.* But this was never written.

She worked fitfully at the Avignon story in the next two years; but her right hand was so troublesome, became instantly so painful when she tried to write, that she was unable to make much headway. It was a story of large design, and needed concentrated vigour and power. Her knowledge of this often led her to put it aside entirely and try to forget about it until better times should come.

The second summer at Northeast Harbour she wrote *Before Breakfast;* and the following year her poignant and beautiful story, *The Best Years*. She wrote it for her brother Roscoe, as a reminder of the time when he and she and Douglass were all children together, and slept in the attic of their old house, that was like a "robbers cave." But when she had it finished and ready to send to him, she got a telegram saying he had died in his sleep.

In the last year, it was the little things one lived in; the pleasure of flowers; of a letter from an old friend in Red Cloud, the flying visit of a young niece; of playing, perhaps, Yehudi's recording with Enesco of the Mozart Concerto in D major, made when he was a young boy; immortal youth, singing its lovely song; and one great thing, beyond and above all the rest—the glory of great poetry, filling all the days. She turned almost entirely to Shakespeare and Chaucer that last winter; as if in their company she found her greatest content, best preferred to confront the future.

One felt the future as one feels the almost imperceptible change of light in the sky, or the coming on of a new season. She was never more herself than on the last morning of her life—the morning of April 24th, 1947. Her spirit was as high, her grasp of reality as firm as always. And she had kept that warmth of heart, that youthful, fiery generosity which life so often burns out.

She was a little tired that morning; full of winning courtesy to those around her; fearless, serene—with the childlike simplicity which had always accompanied her greatness; giving and receiving happiness.